SCOTLAND'S
EDGE
Revisited

Photography and Text by

Keith Allardyce

HarperCollins*Publishers*

T o the many kind people of the Scottish and Manx coasts who helped me in so many ways during my journey for this book, I wish to say a heart felt thank you.

And I would especially like to say thank you to the '84' crew in Edinburgh: Captain James Taylor, Ian Webster, Lorna Grieve and Jack Ross. Thanks are also due to Richard Townsley, Jim Oliver and the Trustees of Scotland's Lighthouse Museum in Fraserburgh for all their help and for giving me the privilege of re-visiting the people of Scotland's edge.

KEITH ALLARDYCE
MARCH 1998

HarperCollins Publishers
P.O. Box, Glasgow G4 0NB

Published in association with Scotland's Lighthouse Museum
with financial assistance from the Kinnaird Head Trust

First published 1998

ISBN 0 00 472194 2

Reprint 9 8 7 6 5 4 3 2 1 0

© Kinnaird Head Trust, 1998

Printed and bound in Italy by Rotolito Lombarda S.p.A., Pioltello

CONTENTS

CONTENTS CONTINUED

This book pays tribute to the remarkable men and women who for over 200 years maintained a proud tradition of lightkeeping which goes back to the origins of the Northern Lighthouse Board in 1786, and back to the men who tended the coal-fired lights on the Isle of May two centuries earlier.

Time moves on. The coal-fired lights gave way to paraffin, to gas, and in turn to solar power. Radio aids and satellite navigation supplement the fundamental service provided by the lighthouses. At the end of a 30-year programme of automation, permanent manning has now given way to Attendants, maintenance teams, and monitoring from the Board's Headquarters in Edinburgh.

These pictures bear witness to the end of a remarkable way of life, and to the many families in which lightkeeping as a tradition was handed down from generation to generation.

Those who remain in its service know that the Northern Lighthouse Board has changed, and will never be quite the same again. It will be for them to maintain the record of reliability and service which the Keepers gave, and to ensure that the Mariner, at sea, and everyone whose business is the sea around Scotland and the Isle of Man can continue to rely on these lights as he has always done in the past.

Anne

Peace and her huge invasion to these shores
Puts daily home; innumerable sails
Dawn on the far horizon and draw near;
Innumerable loves, uncounted hopes
To our wild coasts, not darkling now, approach:

Not now obscure, since thou and thine are there,
And bright on the lone isle, the foundered reef,
The long, resounding foreland, Pharos stands

ROBERT LOUIS STEVENSON
from *To My Father*

INTRODUCTION

I visited my first lighthouse at Kinnaird Head, Fraserburgh in March 1995 when I became manager of Scotland's Lighthouse Museum but since then I have been able to visit most of the lighthouses in Scotland. It might seem strange to be appointed to run the only museum in Scotland entirely dedicated to telling the story of the country's lighthouses without ever having visited one before but at least I had worked in plenty of museums. Kinnaird Head is an excellent place for a lighthouse museum. Not only is there plenty of space in the new building to display the extensive collection of lighthouse artefacts, we also have the jewel in the crown, Kinnaird Head Lighthouse itself which is now a unique example of what a lighthouse in Scotland looked like before automation and the loss of our keepers.

At Scotland's Lighthouse Museum three things struck me very quickly and very forcibly. The first was the commitment and enthusiasm of everyone involved with the museum, particularly all our trustees, the local authorities and our staff, most noticeably Jimmy Oliver, the last Principal Lighthouse Keeper at Kinnaird Head. The second was the quiet professionalism and expertise of the Northern Lighthouse Board. They are the people who, since 1786, have been lighting our coasts with extraordinary skill and success. The NLB never fails to impress; from the officers in Headquarters in

George Street, Edinburgh to the most remote boatman, they continue the work in the best tradition established by their forebears. Without the NLB and all their help, we would not have such a fine museum.

The third thing which struck me in those early days at Kinnaird Head was the book *At Scotland's Edge* by Evelyn Hood and Keith Allardyce. For a new boy to lighthouses, it was and is still an excellent read with a good history of the lighthouses in Scotland, followed by Keith's excellent photographs. I was particularly impressed by the photographs. They said so much, not just about the lights themselves but also about the people who looked after them and made them work. *At Scotland's Edge* had been published in 1986 to celebrate the bicentenary of the formation of the NLB but was no longer in print. Happily, the book had hardly dated at all so I was determined to have a reprint. The problem, as always, was money but like so much to do with Scotland's Lighthouse Museum we were lucky.

Banff and Buchan District Council (who had done so much to build the museum) decided in its dying days before local government re-organisation to fund a reprint. The book was reprinted in time for the official opening of the Museum by HRH The Princess Margaret. It sold like the proverbial hot cakes and we have been able to use the proceeds from the reprint to commission this new book. I was

particularly pleased that Keith was able to revisit 'Scotland's Edge' with his camera, and over two summers, supplemented by a number of other trips supported by the NLB, he undertook the most extensive tours of our lighthouses. This book is the end product of these visits, together with over 8,000 slides which now form the backbone of our extensive photographic collection. It is often invidious to single people out for praise when there have been so many who have contributed, not just to this book, but to the whole success of Scotland's Lighthouse Museum. However, I do want to mention particularly a few individuals. Captain James Taylor, the Chief Executive of the Northern Lighthouse Board and all his staff have been consistently excellent throughout, particularly Bill Patterson, Director of Engineering, and Ian Webster, Administration Manager; I know we have a made a lot of work for Ian especially. Thanks are also due to the trustees of Kinnaird Head Trust under the chairmanship of Dan Urquhart who have made a brave decision ordering this book. I should also mention my employers Scotland's Lighthouse Museum Trust and Aberdeenshire Council. James Carney and the staff at HarperCollins Publishers have also contributed in no small way to the project. Finally, there is Keith himself, without whose talent and sheer perseverance this book would not exist.

Scotland has a unique and proud lighthouse heritage. In the year when the last Scottish lighthouse keepers left their post and had their tasks automated, this book is dedicated to the incredible history and bright future of the Northern Lighthouse Board.

RICHARD TOWNSLEY
Scotland's Lighthouse Museum
MARCH 1998

WEST COAST

BUTT OF LEWIS

I sailed on the Cal-Mac ferry, *Lord of the Isles,* across the Minch from Ullapool to Stornoway; then I drove north over the Lewis moors to the most northerly point of the Outer Hebrides, the Butt of Lewis.

After parking at the lighthouse gate, I walked past the 'Lighthouse Closed' sign and knocked on the doors of each of the three light-keepers in turn, but no-one answered.

Nevertheless, I pitched my tent just outside the garden wall, having cleared the ground first of a dozen or two of rejected tomatoes, thrown over from the keepers' greenhouse on the other side. Then I drove back to the Port of Ness, and phoned the lighthouse: 'You're welcome!' said Donald Michael, the Principal Lighhouse Keeper (PLK). 'Come over right away.

'I'll meet you in the watch-room.' Later I met Donald's wife Greta in their home, and over cups of tea and scones they told me of their thoughts on the future and the past. 'We wouldn't have changed a thing in this life that we've had in the service – we'd do it all over again if we could,' said Greta. We've loved moving home every four or five years too. Our first light was the Flannans – I remember the beautiful view of Loch Roeg from the shore station. Mind you, the move from Aberdeen to Braesclete, the shore station, was special! We took the North Boat to Kirkwall, and were met there by someone with a coal-lorry to take us and our possessions over to the other side, to Stromness. Then we sailed on the Pole Star to Stornoway, where a keeper met us – he was Norrie Muir. The first thing he said to us on the pier was, 'You haven't got a piano, have you?' We were to live on the first floor of the shore-station which had a very narrow staircase.

'So the end of an era is almost here,' I said to Greta. 'In fact it's already ended, hasn't it?' I added. She replied, 'It's a terrible sadness… very sad. I just hate to think about the end. We support what you're doing with this book. At least some people in the future will get a glimpse of what the lighthouse life was like.'

When the Butt closes, Donald will be retired anyway, but Greta said, 'I know we'll need to be near the sea – perched on a cliff somewhere. We'll need a view of the sea.'

Established	1862
Automated	1998
Engineer	David A. Stevenson
Character	Flashing white every 5 seconds
Range	25 miles

I also met Eric Bruce, one of the Assistant Keepers at the Butt, and his wife Rosie. (I knew them from twenty years earlier when I was a Roving Keeper stationed at Corsewall.) 'I never have my photograph taken,' shrieked Rosie, all excited and wobbly. 'Never.' But I was privileged enough later to take a portrait of her with Eric at the tower door. Eric was soon in full swing about his life out here: 'And when I'm not throwing duff tomatoes at your tent, I'm the chairman of the Ness Social Club, I'm secretary of the Port of Ness Harbour Association, I'm the sub-editor of the Paipearnis, I'm the groundsman of the Port of Ness football club, and I'm the secretary of the NLB's Health and Safety Committee. And I'm a light-keeper, don't forget...'

Then there is the First Occasional Light-keeper to the Butt of Lewis, Calum Mackay, a man of Ness. He's also a weaver and a crofter, and every year spends two weeks with nine other men of Ness on the remote Sula Sgeir, forty miles north of the lighthouse, to harvest fat gugas, young gannets, from their nests. Thousands of the gugas are brought back, cleaned and salted, to the Port of Ness every August, where the local people queue up to collect their annual quota of the delicacy. The freezer at the lighthouse engine-room is stocked with a few gugas on Calum's return – 'And sheep's heads – he loves sheep's heads!' says Eric. 'He fills the freezer with them as well!'

Donald Michael PLK

11

ARNISH POINT

The former Attendant Keeper to Arnish Point Lighthouse lives just outside Stornoway. He is John McDonald, a Lewis man, with a life-time connection with the Lighthouse Board.

I found his house – I knew it was the right one, with a typical NLB sundial plinth just outside the back door (salvaged from Arnish Point) – and I spent a wonderful day with him and his wife.

Returning to Lewis after the war in 1945, John had no interest in working at the croft or the loom. After his devastating war-time experiences, he felt he needed to be somehow 'in the open'. As a prisoner-of-war in Germany and Poland, he had spent several months in a salt-mine. Later, on a gruelling march to another camp, a bombing raid left him almost completely deaf.

But on a railway station during the journey, John was so severly beaten on his head with a rifle-butt by a German guard that he almost died instantly, and to this day the injury can still cause him tremendous pain.

Back in Lewis, John answered an advertisement in the Stornoway paper for light-keepers. He was taken on by the NLB and given a brief training at the Butt of Lewis.

His first appointment was as Assistant Keeper at the Pentland Skerries, one of the Orkney lights. In John's time, this was a family station, with plenty of space for livestock and gardens. But apart from the lighthouse crew, there was no-one.

John found it difficult to settle. The last straw came one balmy summer's night when he heard, drifting over the sea, the sound of merriment and dance music. He spied through his telescope the bright lights of the community hall on the neighbouring island, Stroma. A resignation letter was written there and then.

Established	1852
Automated	1963
Engineer	Alan Stevenson
Character	Flashing white/red every 10 sec
Range	White 19 miles, red 15 miles

The Board replied that instead of accepting his resignation, they could offer him a shore-station post. And when John declined, the superintendant (a persistent man, fortunately), asked if he would consider being a Relieving Keeper. This sounded fine to John, and in the next seven months he saw seven lights.

Then the post of Occasional Keeper came up, which John took, at the Flannans – one month on the rock, and two months off. This was ideal as it was home territory, and it was at the Flannans Shore Station that John met his wife, Jessie.

The Flannans were special to John; his father was one of the workmen who built the lighthouse. Jessie brought out an album, and showed me a photograph of all the workmen and a pony grouped beside the lighthouse just before the keepers were to take over.

The building took three working seasons to complete. And when the time came for the site to be cleared and tidied up, the contractor planned to take the pony to the cliff edge and push the animal over. (Every item of the lighthouse, from the stone blocks to the vast optics, was heaved across the island by that pony over those three seasons.)

But John's father refused to let the animal be so cruelly treated. He insisted that it should be allowed to live on, so the pony was led to the landing where it was blindfolded, lifted in a sling, and gently lowered into the service-boat, and returned to the Lewis pastures for retirement.

Top *Former Attendant Keeper John McDonald*
Bottom *Notice to Mariners, Arnish Point*

HASKEIR
GASKER & MONACH

As a consequence of the Donaldson Report, following the wreck of the *Braer* oil tanker on Shetland in 1993, these three new lights are being constructed on the western shores of the Outer Hebrides. They will contribute to the protection of the Scottish coast from further oil-tanker groundings and pollution. The Haskeir light is a major solar/wind-powered light, watched by the computerised monitor centre at the Northern Lighthouse Board HQ in Edinburgh (known to all in the service by its George Street number '84'). Gasker and Monach are minor lights.

On the morning of Sunday 1st June 1997, I arrived at the Oban Depot to join the *Pharos* – we departed at noon on a working trip to Haskeir, Gasker and Monach. Having sailed through the Sound of Mull, out past Ardnamurchan Point and across the Sea of the Hebrides, we anchored off Barra near Castlebay's island castle.

A dozen of the crew went ashore, some to visit relations, others to visit the pub. I looked around Castlebay with my camera; a plaque on the Royal Bank of Scotland read 'Commemorating the Centenary of Cinema 1996 – Alexander 'Sandy' Mackendrick (1912–1993), Film Director who made *Whisky Galore* here in Barra'.

On returning to the work-boat in the harbour, I found Ralph, one of the crew, sitting in the stern, 'on guard'. He was missing out on the pub visit with his mates, so I stood in for him – for over three hours!

The next morning, we sailed for Haskeir to deliver building materials, mainly for the control room. The tower itself is almost complete. Six workmen were delivered to the island with Ian Young, the clerk of works from '84', to start a three-week building stint. The foreman, from

Established	1997
Automated	Built as automatic
Engineer	Bob McIntosh
Character	Flashing white
Range	23 ml (H); 10 ml (G & M)

Glasgow, had a Fathers' Day present and card with him – to be opened later, on the day.

The following day, 3rd June, we sailed for the tiny island of Gasker to tidy up the building site and remove all the left-over materials, as the light is almost complete. As the helicopter lifted the Portaloo, a great shower of water sprayed us all, at first giving us a shock until we realised it was just the header-tank supply.

This is a dainty and green little island. Every time the helicopter arrived from the ship, about fifty greylag geese flew up and circled us, honking, before quickly settling again to graze on the lush turf.

Later in the afternoon, Ian, Peter Fleming (an engineer from '84'), and myself were landed by helicopter at the Monach Islands, a twenty-minute flight south. Ian and Peter gave the old Monach a building inspection – the light was switched off and abandoned in 1942. We carefully looked around the keeper's quarters, and in the gloom could make out the superb craftsmanship of the woodwork – the pine-panelled staircase and doors and window-shutters. Up the tower itself, the optics, cold for over half a century, stood under a decaying shroud. A tiny temporary light on a low scaffolding stood near the base of the tower, in use until the minor light is constructed.

An extract from NLB Journal ('Works in Progress' article) reads:

A temporary light has operated at Monach Island since 31st August 1996. Tenders have been invited for a low maintenance aluminium lattice structure and these are expected shortly. It may be necessary to delay construction of the permanent light at Monach until the black guillemots have completed their nesting phase. It will also be necessary to construct a fence around the light in order to keep the seals away.

Top *Inside the old light at Monach, first lit in 1864*
Bottom *The extinct Monach Lighthouse, decommissioned in 1942*

BARRA HEAD & SGEIR LEAHD

On a calm mid-September morning, I sailed on the *Lord of the Isles* ferry from Loch Boisdale to Castlebay on Barra. I'd been up before sunrise, long before the ferry departed, and from the pier saw a magical display of lights – the harbour lights, and beyond, two buoys, and the minor lights of Gasey Island and Calvay – flashing against a sky of vivid pinks and purples. Then suddenly, after no more than ten minutes, the lights switched themselves off as the daylight increased, the sky turned pale grey, and the magic vanished.

At Castlebay, I found a B & B run by Annie McNeil. She asked if I'd travelled all the way down the Western Isles. When I explained that I had, and that I was hoping to complete my journey to Barra Head Lighthouse, she told me that it was a curious coincidence that I should have found her B & B. She went on, 'My father was a

keeper at Barra Head. But he had a terrible accident there in 1965. He fell on the stairs in the tower, and fractured his skull, and he died there.'

The day I arrived in Castlebay, the weather began to get worse. For the following week, continuous gales were forecast from the south, the worst direction for me. I couldn't wait at Castlebay for so long, so instead I visited one of the minor lights near Vatersay with the Attendant Keeper, John Allen McNeil. (He is the Attendant to five minor lights on this side of Barra, and is the observer and boatman to Barra Head Lighthouse.)

So we went to Sgeir Leadh, (the Blue Rock), on one of John's regular visits to check the light. His little boat just made it in the choppy seas, and we nosed into a sheltered cleft beside the lighthouse.

We jumped ashore, and I took some portraits of John

moments before the sun's last rays dropped below the horizon.

By chance, the following year, I had an opportunity to photograph Barra Head Lighthouse from the NLB helicopter. The MV *Pharos*, with the helicopter, was on her way to Uist when a slight detour was made, to pick up three workmen from Barra Head who had spent about two weeks at the lighthouse.

Barra Head

Established	1833
Automated	1980
Engineer	Robert Stevenson
Character	Flashing white every 3 seconds
Range	8 miles

USHENISH

Top *Ushenish lighthouse from the air*
Right *Iain McLeod at the lighthouse*

I found Iain McLeod, the Attendant to the Ushenish light for around 20 years, outside the Loch Skipport shop. We made an arrangement to visit Ushenish with his two boatmen the following day.

We took a ten-minute drive to the jetty, and then a motor-boat for over three-quarters of an hour; then we reached a little shingle beach in a sheltered bay. Above the beach, Iain kept his 1958 Ford Dexter tractor, gleaming in a recent coat of blue paint, in a grand NLB shed. We then took the tractor, with a trailer for me to sit in, over the moors for about twenty minutes.

Arriving at the lighthouse was a bit of an anti-climax really. The tower looked neat with the engineer's plaque above the door, and a white wall surrounded the grounds. But the keepers' cottages were gone, demolished during the automation programme, and only their foundations could be seen.

'You must have had some rough journeys to the light in your time?' I said to Iain, when we got back to Loch Skipport. Iain looked away for a moment, before turning to tell me, 'Well, the worst journey I've ever had was when I got all the way to the lighthouse door and discovered that I'd forgotten to pick up the key.'

I met Iain again the following summer, when I was sailing with the *Pharos*, returning from the Gasker, Haskeir and Monach trip. He was being delivered, by helicopter, a brand new six-wheel 'Gator', a six-wheel buggy, to replace the magnificent blue tractor. After a ten-minute demonstration and a try-out, Iain looked as if he wanted to be alone, so we climbed back on board the helicopter and returned to the ship.

Established	1857
Automated	1970
Engineer	David & Thomas Stevenson
Character	Flashing white/red every 20 sec
Range	White 19 miles, red 15 miles

NEIST POINT

The last time I visited Neist Point Lighthouse was in November 1983. Three keepers lived here then when this was a Rock Station. On that visit I parked at the keepers' car park on a high crag above the tower. My girl friend was with me at the time, and we ran all the way down the long path to the light, and got soaked in a gale, lashing rain and hail.

Now, in the summer, thirteen years later, tourists have parked their cars at the craggy car park. A notice board advertises Bed and Breakfast and self-catering accommodation at the lighthouse. Even the old engine-room, which once housed three great Kelvin diesel generators for the fog-horn, has been stripped bare and converted into accommodation.

Near the tower, there is a 'grave yard' of about two dozen fibre glass tombstones. They were left behind by a film company after making the film *Breaking the Waves*. Another notice board tells me that this film won the silver medal at the 1996 Cannes Film Festival.

I met Calum MacLeod, an ex-Neist keeper, near the lighthouse. He was one of the last three keepers. 'We locked the doors behind us and walked up the hill on the last day, and never looked back. It was a sad day. The job was the best I've ever had – I miss it.' Before the last keepers left the light, they worked with technicians from '84' to strip the lantern and the light-room of the old optics and winding gear. It was on its way to Edinburgh, and has since been installed at Scotland's Lighthouse Museum in Fraserburgh.

'It could be a problem with getting our stores out here,' said Calum. 'We used a Bedford barrow to carry everything down the long path from the car park. A gale once blew one of the store boxes off the barrow. The box flew up in a spectacular curve and landed in the sea. But it was found later by a local fisherman - he phoned us to say "I've found Sandy's pyjamas!" '

Above *Neist Point light*
Below *Attendant Keeper, Neil Carter*

Established	1909
Automated	1990
Engineer	David A. Stevenson
Character	Flashing 2 white every 5 sec
Range	16 miles

ARDTRECK
KYLEAKIN, PORT ELLEN & McARTHUR'S HEAD

Ardtreck

Angie Bain is the tour guide at Skye's famous Talisker whisky distillery, and she is Attendant Keeper to the Ardtreck minor light. She took over as Attendant from her mother, who in turn took over from her father who was the first Attendant, starting in 1939. I went to Ardtreck with Angie and her husband, Kenny, on their fortnightly check of the light.

They usually go together – it's near their cottage – to check the gas pressure, the gas mantle and the cylinder-room temperature. Once a year, they lovingly paint the tower themselves, inside and out. Kenny also works at the distillery – it is his touch of magic as the Still-man which gives their single malt its distinctive character.

Established	1904
Automated	Built as automatic
Engineer	–David A. Stevenson
Character	Isophase white every 5 seconds
Range	16 miles

Kyleakin

I photographed Kyleakin Lighthouse from the deck of the *Fingal* as we sailed south through the narrows between Eilean Ban (the White Island) and Skye. The new Skye Bridge cuts right across Eilean Ban, and reaches high over the lighthouse and keepers' cottages. The light was made obsolete with the construction of the bridge.

The extraordinary beauty and magic of Eilean Ban has been devastated by the bridge and the road. I could hardly believe that such a destructive project would have been ever contemplated. There was even a suggestion to demolish the lighthouse – an 1857 masterpiece built by Robert Louis Stevenson's father and uncle.

Established	1857
Automated	1960
Engineer	David & Thomas Stevenson
Character	Discontinued
Range	Light now on the bridge

When I first visited the island, long before the bridge, it felt like another world, so close to the tourist route, and yet so cut off from it.

Gavin Maxwell lived here for a short time, after the light's automation, until his death in 1969. In *Raven Seek Thy Brother*, Maxwell tells of the island's haunting: 'A keeper was on the island for seven years, and during that time became so accustomed to the voices and the metallic clang that he came simply to ignore them.'

Port Ellen

The village of Port Ellen on Islay was built in the 1820s by Walter Frederick Campbell, a wealthy landowner, and named after his first wife, Lady Ellinor.

After her death, he built this memorial tower and beacon across the bay from the village in 1832. And he sings her praises on a large marble plaque above the door in 21 lines of flowery verse. I lost my copy of this verse on my travels, so I then wrote to Port Ellen's tourist office to ask for help. It turned out that there was no tourist office, so it was given to Thomas Thomson of the village who kindly went to the tower to jot down the verse. He noted in his letter to me that he was uncertain of one or two of the words in the verse: 'I'm not totally sure of this, but clinging to the rock in a force 7 gale, this is the best I could do.'

> *'Ye, who mid storms and tempests stray*
> *In danger's midnight hour,*
> *Behold where shines this friendly ray*
> *And hail its guardian power.*
> *'Tis but faint emblem of her light*
> *My fond and faithful guide… '*

McArthur's Head

I passed McArthur's Head on the *Pharos* sailing from Oban and through the Sound of Islay. The station sits on a steep hillside on Islay – at the eastern end of the Sound of Jura.

Jim Oliver, (now Assistant Manager of Scotland's Lighthouse Museum), was posted to McArthur's Head for six weeks as a Supernumerary, very soon after joining the service: 'I arrived at McArthur's Head on Christmas Day 1965,' says Jim. 'It was the last of the two-man stations in Scotland. Well, first of all I got to the Port Askaig Hotel on Christmas Eve. There was a power cut in Islay at the time – so I was given a candle and had my dinner on my own that evening. Then the next day Dougie the boatman took me to the light. I climbed the steps up to the cliff – the light stands about 200 feet above sea level, but the Blondin took my cases. It was the bleakest damn joint I ever stayed in! But that was mainly because of the PLK. He'd made a paraffin lamp out of a sweetie jar with a metal lid and a wick and chimney on top. That was the heater for my room. The PLK said that I couldn't light a coal fire in my quarters – he'd put a board over my fire place and painted on it a heap of coal with flames and smoke !'

Opposite *Ardtreck Lighthouse*
Top *Port Ellen Lighthouse*
Middle *Kyleakin Lighthouse and the Skye bridge*
Bottom *McArthur's Head Lighthouse*

Established	1861
Automated	1969
Engineer	David & Thomas Stevenson
Character	Flashing 2 white/red every 10 sec
Range	White 14 miles, red 11 miles

MV FINGAL & OBAN DEPOT

MV *Fingal* in the Cromarty Firth

Saturday 8th Feb 1997: I boarded the Fingal at Oban's NLB Depot pier at around 21.00 hours. Met Captain Alan Rør, and the Chief Steward Les Flett showed me to my bunk – State Room A. A notice on the door read 'Lady in Waiting' – my cabin was next door to State Room B, the Patron's cabin. After a night of gales – worrying for me as I easily get seasick – I awoke to peer out over Oban Bay on a calm, clear morning.

Sunday 9th Feb 1997: Sailed south from Oban down the Firth of Lorne to the Sound of Gigha where two buoys were to be gauged (between Gigha and the Mull of Kintyre). As the wind was rising, and forecast for gale force, we found shelter for the night off Salen in the Sound of Mull.

Monday 10th Feb 1997: Departed Sound of Mull at 08.00 hours, and rounded Ardnamurchan Point, heading north through the Sound of Sleat. Snow lay on the mountain tops on each side. The day is cold, windy and showery. We anchored again, in the shelter of Broadford Bay.

Tuesday 11th Feb 1997: After a very stormy night, the weather suddenly calmed by the time breakfast was over. We sailed for the two buoys, one just north, and one just south, of the new Skye Bridge. Each buoy, gas-powered, was swapped with a new solar-powered buoy. As we turned to approach the secured buoy in the Sound of Sleat, a flock of about 200 eiders thrashed the sea in front of us in a spectacular panic to avoid the ship's path. With the mission completed, we sailed south to head back to the Oban Depot. But just as we were passing Isle Ornsay light, halfway through the Sound of Sleat, the second engineer suddenly remembered that he hadn't connected a vital contact in the first of the new solar buoys.

The captain ordered a sudden U-turn.

The Oban Depot

The west coast of Scotland base for the NLB lies at Oban, on the south side of the bay. There is a pier for the NLB ships, a helicopter pad, and workshops, stores, and an office. It was from Oban that light-keepers were taken by ship to some of Scotland's remotest rocks. By the time I visited Oban for this book, only two west coast Rock Lights were still manned (and serviced from this depot): the Rhinns of Islay and Hyskeir.

Opposite page *MV* Fingal

Above *A well-earned rest*

Left and below Fingal's *crew at work in the Sound of Sleat, Skye*

HYSKEIR

I had waited a long time for an opportunity to visit Hyskeir. Having first glimpsed it in the early 1970s from Harris Bay on Rhum, about 15 miles distant, I had become curious about it. But I knew nothing of light-houses then, and didn't even know its name. But something about it fascinated me.

A little later, I would hear about Hyskeir from light-keepers when I was a Roving Relief Keeper. Then I read a reference to it in Gavin Maxwell's book, *Harpoon at a Venture*, where he wrote that keepers had told him of basking sharks swimming right under them as they stood on a small bridge which links two of the reefs.

But now, in late summer of 1996, I had an opportunity to visit Hyskeir with Ian Young, the Board's Clerk of Works. We took the half-hour helicopter flight from Oban, and spent four hours on the island while Ian examined the building, alterations and painting work.

For me, it was too late, really. The magic of the place had gone with the arrival of the portacabins and extra electricity generators, and with all the noise.

The keepers said they were merely caterers now, catering for the groups of builders, technicians and painters until automation work is complete. They had even given up their famous vegetable gardens – each keeper had his own plot, and there was a shared one called the Rock Garden. The Rock Garden was made famous when it featured in a television cookery programme.

Established	1904
Automated	1997
Engineer	David A. Stevenson
Character	Flashing 3 white every 30 sec
Range	24 miles

Now, the gardens lay abandoned. I photographed the three keepers in the Rock Garden – a small forest of carrots, onions and cabbages, all gone to seed – a strange oasis in the island wilderness.

Alan Crowe was the last PLK to leave Hyskeir Lighthouse, when the station was automated in January 1997. His family have been connected with the Northern Lights for over 200 years: 'My earliest ancestors in the service were builders and boatmen at the Pentland Skerries twin-lights. Some later became keepers when the building was completed.'

'Jim Cummings was an ancestor of mine who was a stone-mason at Skerryvore, and he later became the first keeper there. So my father and grandfather were keepers too… Hyskeir was the kind of station you regretted leaving. It was a happy station, a nice island. In the summer it was absolutely fantastic. I used to fish for lobsters out there, and you know about our gardens. We had a TV crew out there once, when I made a carrot casserole for the Sophie Grigson cookery programme.

'On my last day, the three of us took off in the helicopter to leave the light. I had a lump in my throat when I took one last look at the island – just a little dot in the ocean which I'd never see again…'

Top *Ian Young, Clerk-of-Works*
Bottom *The fortnightly relief*

ARDNAMURCHAN

This was the nearest I got to Ardnamurchan Light-house on my journey – on my return helicopter from Hyskeir with the Clerk of Works to Oban. Ardnamurchan is Scotland's westernmost mainland point. Back in 1983, I stayed at the lighthouse for two nights, photographing for *At Scotland's Edge*. It was a family station then; and the tower still had the original fixed optics, with a revolving cylinder in which were two slits through which the light shone to be magnified by the lens.

In August 1986, HM the Queen and other members of the Royal Family disembarked from *Britannia* on their annual cruise to visit Ardnamurchan Lighthouse. The occasion was the NLB's 200th anniversary. During the visit, the Queen met Sam and Nadeje Neighbour as they stood at the door of their lorry-home. Sam was one of the last of the roving light-keepers – though he wasn't able to rove too far with his slow, lumbering lorry. But the lorry could be 'plugged in' to whichever mainland lighthouse Sam was posted to.

I first met Sam at Noss Head, when we were both rov-ing keepers. While Sam was stationed at Noss Head for months, I spent only two weeks there before being ordered by '84' to be taken by helicopter to Sule Skerry at a moment's notice.

The original optics and winding gear and the light-room paraphernalia of Ardnamurchan are now on display in the former PLK's house, while the engine-room and the sta-ble block have been converted into a visitor centre by Highland Council. The two assistant keepers' houses are now available for lets.

Established	1849
Automated	1988
Engineer	Alan Stevenson
Character	Flashing 2 white every 20 sec
Range	24 miles

HYNISH

The *Pharos* dropped anchor off Tiree – on return from the outer Isles. With Captain Willie Tulloch and most of the crew, we took the work-boat to Tiree's tiny harbour at Scarinish. From there, Willie and I set off to cycle the seven miles to Hynish Signal Tower, while the crew headed for the bar of the Scarinish Hotel.

Accompanied all the way by singing skylarks under a deep blue sky, we cycled past acres of buttercups and clover during the last hour or so of sunlight. A corn-crake rasped from a patch of yellow irises as we approached the tower.

We arrived at the signal tower just in time for me to photograph it before the daylight faded too much, while Willie explored inside the tower and read about the Skerryvore story.

The Hynish Signal tower was originally used by the 'ashore' Skerryvore keepers to communicate with the 'on the rock' keepers before the introduction of radio telephones. It was renovated by my friend Mike Stanfield, the founder and director of the Hebridean Trust; and inside the tower he has established the Skerryvore Museum. Mike wrote to me to explain his enthusiasm for the Hynish project:

'I determined that this story should not fade into obscurity alongside the modern technological achievements of the space age… The Skerryvore Lighthouse is 138 feet high, made up of 97 courses of granite, in total 58,000 cubic feet. Each course was laid out at the Shore Station of Hynish, on the foundations of what is now the Signal Tower, some twelve miles by sea from the Skerryvore Rocks, and carefully fitted together, so that when the tower was complete nowhere was the diameter more than 1/16 of an inch out of true. Indeed an architectural wonder of the world.'

DUBH ARTACH

The *Pharos* dropped anchor off Dubh Artach at 6.00 am on 5th June 1997 on the way to Ushenish from the Uists. The helicopter delivered supplies of fuel and water from the ship.

Three technicians were staying on the rock for two weeks: Jim Downs, Project Engineer, and Mike Samuel, Electrical Technician, from '84', and an electrical contractor from Oban.

'It's no home – no showers, no room to move,' said Jim. (One translation of Dubh Artach is 'black and dismal'.)

I was last here in 1983. The gas cylinders were being changed then. Now the old watch-room is packed with computers, and a bank of solar panels sits on the balcony. A 3" high 35 watt bulb forms the illumination in a Dalen lens, and has a range of twenty nautical miles.

Waiting to return to the ship later that June morning, I stood with the granite tower at my back. Before me, the helicopter pad sat where the original Dubh Artach workmen had their iron barracks, on long legs, when they built the tower, block by block, in the 1870s. And I imagined, as I always do when I think of Dubh Artach, the foreman builder. Robert Louis Stevenson wrote of him: 'Mr Goodwillie, whom I see before me still in his rock habit of indecipherable rags, would get his fiddle down and strike up human minstrelsy amid the music of the storm.'

Above *Mike Samuel, electrical technician*

Established	1872
Automated	1971
Engineer	David & Thomas Stevenson
Character	Flashing 2 white every 30 sec
Range	20 miles

LISMORE

I joined Donald Morrison, Lismore's Attendant, at Oban Depot where we took a 25-foot 'rib' out to the lighthouse for one of the fortnightly checks. Within minutes we were in the wide blue Firth of Lorne before entering the Sound of Mull with its imposing monuments, the dark and dramatic Duart Castle on Mull to the west, and the gleaming white Lismore Lighthouse on Eilean Musdile to the east. Donald first checked the minor lights of Lady Rock and Grey Rocks before landing at Lismore. We surprised an old man at the lighthouse, who was looking after the cottages for the summer. He had reclaimed a corner of the garden from the knee-high grass within the high sheltering walls.

After the usual checks in the lantern, Donald entered the quarterdeck to check the gas cylinders: one summer bank of ten, one winter bank of twenty, and one reserve of five cylinders.

The lighthouse is due to be modernised with solar panels in 2001.

Below *Attendant Keeper Donald Morrison, Lismore*

Established	1833
Automated	1965
Engineer	Robert Stevenson
Character	Flashing white every 10 sec
Range	19 miles

RHINNS OF ISLAY

Unable to find the Rhinns of Islay boatman in Portnahaven (last seen by his neighbour walking up the road and out of the village), I went over to a fishing boat tied to the harbour jetty. Fortunately, the fisherman agreed to take me over to the Rhinns – a five-minute trip. Arriving at the Rhinns, we passed close to a dozen common seals hauled onto a rock – almost ignoring our presence.

Alan Rankin, the Second Assistant, met me at the jetty, and we walked to the lighthouse with all my baggage – I was staying for two nights. At the light, I met John Kermode, the PLK, and Bill Crockett, the First Assistant.

I knew John from my time as keeper at Sule Skerry Lighthouse in the late 1970s. When he was first stationed

Established	1825
Automated	1998
Engineer	Robert Stevenson
Character	Flashing white every 5 seconds
Range	24 miles

at the Rhinns, in 1976, the light was fuelled on paraffin. The system worked on the same principle as a tilly lamp. The optical system was then a 3-ton set of lenses and prisms set in bronze. The whole thing revolved through the night, needing to be wound every 45 minutes.

Apart from the usual work which applied to all keepers, keeping the place clean and tidy, and painting, John's work included taking meteorological readings every day and sending the information via radio-telephone to the nearest mainland meteorological office in Stranraer.

Now, in September 1996, the keepers' work at the Rhinns has changed dramatically. The optics (now in Scotland's Lighthouse Museum) have been replaced with a sealed beam unit of two banks of eight lamps. The unit revolves automatically, and should a fault occur in a set of lamps, then another set switches into place.

The meteorological reports, now 'synoptic and NCM' says John, are transmitted by computer directly to the Met. Office headquarters in Bracknell.

Every six hours, a keeper has to check the accuracy of the radio-beacon; this device automatically transmits a code-signal for use as a navigational aid for shipping within a radius of 70 nautical miles. There is a satellite receiver and transmitter, components of a system which also provides accurate position-finding for shipping.

In spite of being surrounded by sophisticated electronic gadgetry, the keepers at the Rhinns continue to be keen gardeners. The old walled garden on the island is well used, and the main harvest was just about to begin. The day after I left, barrow-loads of vegetables were due to be harvested and packed, ready for loading into the helicopter before the relief to Oban.

Above *Alan Rankin, Assistant Keeper*

Above *John Kermode, PLK*

TOWARD POINT

I drove down from Dunoon one late afternoon to visit Toward Point. The lighthouse switched itself on while I set up my tripod and camera in the dusk. A group of seals on the shore behind me snorted and wailed. Some people, staying in the former keepers' quarters below the tower, peered out of their windows.

I later wrote to the Clyde Port Authority (who now call themselves Clydeport) for more information about Toward – it's not one of the NLB lights. They sent me a copy of a book, written on the Clyde Lights, earlier this century by a George Blake:

> Toward is a pleasant place, popular with the keepers and their families. The triangle of pastoral country under the hills has a gentle charm, and gardens flourish in the mild western air. Access to the schools and shops of Innellan and Dunoon is easy by bus, but a sweet sense of remoteness lingers about the white pillar that looks serenely up and down the Firth…

The light from Toward first shone over the waters in 1812, when Britain was engaged in a nasty little war with the States of America, and Napoleon was embarked on the expedition into Russia that gave Tchaikovsky the inspiration for a thunderous overture…

A quaint little building in front, rather like a Wee Free Kirk in the remote Highlands, houses the machinery for compressing air for the foghorn.

Established	1812
Automated	1974
Engineer	Robert Stevenson
Character	Flashing white every 10 sec
Range	22 miles

HOLY ISLAND

There was an hour to go before sunset. And on a little promontory on Arran, opposite Holy Island's 'Wee Donald' minor lighthouse, I set my camera on a tripod. The air was perfectly still. Restless seagulls, calling and flying around their hillside roost further down the shore, temporarily disturbed the silence. The sky turned a pewter colour. 'Wee Donald' flashed its dark green light, a dash of colour in a wide panorama of dark mountain, sea and sky. I photographed the magical landscape.

A little later, at exactly seven o'clock, the sound of a drum and chanting carried over the water from behind the lighthouse. The daylight faded rapidly, and heavy rain sent me running for shelter.

The next day, Harry Walker, Holy Island's Attendant Keeper and Boatman, took me to the Outer Light, a large, square tower just around the corner from 'Wee Donald'. Two painters were there, Jack Marshall and his son Darren, occupying the first floor; I stayed in the second floor, immediately below the light-room, for three nights.

Jack has been painting the towers of the Northern Lights for around twenty years. His first tower was Sule Skerry, where he worked in the summer with his brother and two other men. The job went well, except for an incident at Duncan's Rock, one of the island's jetties. Walking back from the jetty one day, Jack and one of his workmates were swept off the path and winded by a huge wave. They were saved by hanging onto the railing chains.

Here at Holy Island's Outer Light, the tower is being given five coats of paint. While I was

Left *Holy Island Outer Light*

Established	1905
Automated	1977
Engineer	David A. Stevenson
Character	Flashing 2 white every 20 sec
Range	25 miles

Top *Holy Island Inner light*

Above *Inside the Outer Light*

photographing the painters one morning from the top of the tower, we were distracted by the sound of something thrashing around in the sea below us. For several minutes we watched an otter struggle with a huge conger eel, (a foot longer than the otter), before the otter dragged its prey onto the shore. We could even hear the juicy crunching of the eel's head as the otter started to feed.

Jack and Darren, and Jack's brother Bill, painted the famous Bell Rock in 1987, painting inside and out. (Many decades of the outside paint were stripped completely; they discovered a layer of black paint from the war years and they also saw the marks left by machine-gun strafing deep in the granite.) The work lasted six weeks – a thorough job. But two weeks later, Jack heard the news about the fire which devastated the tower. Jack was called back to paint the Bell all over again.

Holy Island has been owned by the Samye Ling Tibetan Centre in Dumfriesshire since 1992, which has established a Buddhist community where meditation

Bottom *Jane Sloan and her sons Guy and Simon (left to right)*

Below *Jack Marshall and son Darren*

and conservation can meet.

The former lighthouse keepers' cottages, above 'Wee Donald', the minor light, have been renovated to provide accommodation for around seven monks and nuns, and seven retreat rooms for visitors.

The engine room, where the three diesel generators once stood, to provide compressed air for the fog-horn, is now a shrine-room. In the room, there is a table covered with a blue cloth, below a yellow wall-hanging depicting four knots of eter nity. On the table, there is a statue of the Buddha, three pictures of deities, and offerings of flowers, candles, incense, bowls of water (yellow with saffron), a shell, and a cake, decorated with gold.

Along the path to the island's north-end jetty, a series of rock faces have been painted by one of the Holy Island nuns. Dechi Wangmo has been painting the rocks to depict Buddhist deities, following her eleven-year art studies at the Samye Ling Centre.

The observer to the Holy Island Outer Light is Jane Sloan of Corrie, near Brodick, on Arran. She used to live on Holy Island, before the lighthouse was automated, and spent three summers as a warden for the University Federation for Animal Welfare.

Jane can see the Outer Light from the doorstep of her home, and her husband has just taken over from the previous Attendant Keeper to Holy Island.

PLADDA

I photographed Pladda shortly after sunset from the hillside above Kildonan on Arran's south side. The lighthouse beams reflected over the bay, and far beyond I saw the flashes of another six major lighthouses, all now automatic, across the wide entrance to the Firth of Clyde.

Four of these lights were part of my life as a Roving Keeper in the 1970s, while I was stationed at Corsewall. From there, our duties were to call, three times a day, the four Rock Stations, Sanda, Pladda, Holy Island and Ailsa Craig, to check the Rock Keepers' well-being and test their radio equipment.

The following day, Hamish MacNeil, Pladda's Attendant Keeper, Observer and Boatman, took me to the island for a day's photography. The Keepers' cottages have been bought by Sally and Derek Morton. They were spending the last day of their summer holiday on Pladda with their son Finn on the day that I arrived.

Sally and Derek were married in Lamlash Registry Office, on Arran, in 1991. 'We had our honeymoon for two weeks on Pladda before the ceremony,' Sally told me, 'and we made a wedding cake in the only dish we had big enough – the dog's bowl.

'Just after the ceremony at Lamlash', Sally continued, 'the Arran Banner photographer burst in and told us to "do this… do that". He took us so much by surprise, we looked like Bonny and Clyde. Then straight after our marriage, we nipped into the Co-op, and bumped into our witnesses that we'd found earlier – and then sped back to Derbyshire.

Left *Sally and Derek Morton with their son, Finn*

Established	1790
Automated	1990
Engineer	Thomas Smith
Character	Flashing 3 white every 30 sec
Range	17 miles

'We spent a lot of our time during our Pladda honeymoon hand-cranking the electric generator, and repairing our water-heater. In fact, Finn was conceived on the very day that our generator broke down altogether.'

Top *The inner staircase*
Bottom *The view from the lower lantern to Ailsa Craig*

TURNBERRY

Turnberry Lighthouse stands right by the 17th hole of the famous Turnberry Golf Course. The tower often presents a background for televised golfing tournaments. I had to go to the luxurious Turnberry Hotel and Spa, which owns the course, for permission to drive across the links (well patrolled by security guards) and wander about the shore.

There was an air of neglect about the lighthouse as the keepers' quarters had been standing empty for a few years. And I thought of the late Andy Sinclair, a PLK who died here, leaving his wife, Kathleen. I had first met Andy at Sule Skerry when I was a Roving Keeper. He was a larger-than-life keeper, always enthusiastic; often he would be working at the workshop lathe, or fishing, or reading, or playing the fiddle.

But Turnberry was an ideal station for Norman Douglas, who is now part of the monitor centre team at '84'. Norman spent his four weeks 'off' at Turnberry (the light was automated by then), and spent his four weeks 'on' over at Ailsa Craig. The light at the Craig was still paraffin, and the Victorian machinery still needed winding every half hour to keep the lens revolving all through the night. Almost overnight, Norman was transferred from the paraffin age to the computerised space-age at '84' and its monitor centre where all the major lights are automatically 'watched' from the centre of Edinburgh.

As Norman was keen on golf and golfers, he welcomed many a visitor on looking around the lighthouse at Turnberry. Consequently, the visitors' book, which he has kept as a souvenir, is full of the names of the rich and famous in the sporting and show-business world.

Established	1873
Automated	1986
Engineer	David & Thomas Stevenson
Character	Flashing white every 15 sec
Range	24 miles

CORSEWALL

During my year as a Roving Keeper in 1975, I was posted to Corsewall Lighthouse for about three weeks. The PLK at that time must have had the smartest station inside, and out, in the whole of Scotland. At the end of one of my watches, a four-hour shift, the PLK pointed out 'a problem' in the engine room. There, at a joint in an oil-pipe which carried diesel to the Kelvin generator, was a drop of oil just waiting to drop onto the floor.

Since automation, the keepers' quarters and the engine room have been sold and converted into a luxury hotel. It was very strange to see the place, with the hotel's own flag flying at the flag-pole, many cars in the car park, and a couple of chefs having a smoke outside the kitchens.

The watch-room is now part of the foyer, and it was from here that the keepers would do 'the speak'– make radio contact with the four Rock Stations in the area, Sanda, Pladda, Holy Island and Ailsa Craig.

But now, the station is called Corsewall Lighthouse Hotel and its brochure tells me: 'Corsewall Lighthouse Hotel invests the charm and romance of an 1815 functioning lighthouse with the comforts of a small, unique luxury hotel and restaurant…

The lighthouse is an 'A'-listed building of major national importance. Its light still beams a warning for ships approaching the mouth of Loch Ryan – as it has done for 180 years.'

Established	1816
Automated	1964
Engineer	Robert Stevenson
Character	Flashing 5 white every 30 sec
Range	22 miles

LITTLE ROSS
&HESTAN ISLAND

George Davidson and a boat-hand took me in their launch to Little Ross Lighthouse. We sailed out of the Kirkcudbright harbour, and followed the River Dee estuary. George is the Attendant and Boatman to Little Ross, and on the way over, he brought up the subject of the tragedy which occurred at the lighthouse in 1960; as he had been the local lifeboat coxswain from 1950 until 1984, George was closely involved with the events.

There had been two keepers stationed at Little Ross Lighthouse at the time of the incident, Hugh Clark and George Dickson. During a sailing trip in the bay, two people had taken shelter for a while beside the island, and had decided to visit the keepers. Unable to find anyone, they returned to the jetty to have a picnic. A little later they returned to the lighthouse where they entered one of the keeper's cottages. They looked in all the rooms until they reached the bedroom of Hugh Clark where they found him obviously dead in bed, murdered with a sawn-off shot-gun.

The other keeper, George Dickson, was by this time heading for Selby in Yorkshire, where he was soon apprehended by the police. (This tragic story ended with George Dickson's suicide.) By the end of the year, the lighthouse had been demanned and automated.

Above *George Davidson*
Opposite Top *The salmon nets at Hestan Island*
Opposite Middle *Eddie and Norman Parker*
Opposite Bottom *Detail, Little Ross*

Established	1843
Automated	1961
Engineer	Alan Stevenson
Character	Flashing white every 5 seconds
Range	12 miles

Hestan Island

It would have been easy to overlook the two lights of the Solway Firth, Little Ross and Hestan Island. I could have driven on through Dumfriesshire and Galloway, and made straight for the major lights along the Rhinns of Galloway. So it was fortunate for me to have found Eddie Parker and his son Norman, the Attendants to Hestan Island Lighthouse.

Eddie started as Attendant Keeper at Hestan in 1957. In those early years he had to visit the light twice a week, when it ran on propane gas. Eddie also used to help on the farm at Hestan Island – the farmer there was Attendant before Eddie: 'His ashes are scattered on Hestan Island,' said Eddie, 'and it won't be long before my ashes are there too!'

Part of Eddie's job is to act as Boatman to Hestan Island, when required by visiting technicians and others from '84'. But when he can, he takes his tractor, and drives over the broad mud-flats of Auchencairn Bay at low tide.

'Hurricane Andrew,' recalled Eddie, 'was one of the old Superintendants of '84', a real company man – all his buttons polished. He came to me and insisted on going by boat to Hestan. It was a Saturday night one January when he told me he wanted to go over the next morning. No matter what I said, we had to go over the next day, even when I told him about the forecast – gales. We got half way over, and Hurricane Andrew called 'Turn Back! Turn Back!' so I said 'No! You insisted on this!', and on we went. Well, at the tower, Hurricane Andrew couldn't even stand up straight – he was wanting to measure up for a new lantern – so we had to head back to the mainland. In fact Hurricane's assistant wanted to spend the night on Hestan, he was so afraid of that sea.

I went to Hestan Island with Eddie and Norman on their tractor – over the flats at low tide (this was after Norman had checked his salmon nets – and found two large salmon).

'No, we can't stop!' called Eddie, when I asked him if I could photograph him and Norman on the tractor in the middle of the bay. I insisted, and got through to Eddie, and reminded him that I had paid them for the trip. So we did stop, I took this portrait, and we continued and reached the island, drove past the old farmhouse and over a small hill, and reached the light. The original

tower had been demolished earlier in the year, and replaced by an aluminium frame supporting the small lamp.

No sooner had we arrived, then Eddie and Norman were anxious to return to base, to beat the tide. 'That was the hardest £20.00 I've ever earned!' said Norman, back at the tractor shed.

Established	1893
Automated	Built as automatic
Engineer	David A. Stevenson
Character	Flashing 2 white every 10 sec
Range	7 miles

MV PHAROS

The eighth and latest *Pharos* to sail the Scottish seas was launched in 1993 at Ferguson's Shipyard on the Clyde. She has a length of almost 78 metres, a draught of almost 4 metres, and has a crew of 23 who work on a one-month-on and one-month-off rota.

The ship is therefore shared between two crews and two captains. And after a month's work, she usually returns to Oban for the crew change-over. Last year, she covered 18,000 nautical miles. Fitted with an integrated bridge system using radar and electronic charts and a satellite navigational aid, she could automatically cruise from Oban around to Leith if initially fed the appropriate data.

'But the biggest single improvement,' says Captain David Davidson, 'is the big helicopter deck.' Helicopter work using the old *Pharos* could be very dangerous, as the modification to the stern for the helicopter pad was far from ideal.

The new *Pharos* services the lighthouses on what are called 'blitzing' trips. Working with the helicopter, supplies of diesel, gas cylinders, new electrical equipment and building materials, and a host of other odds and ends can be delivered to the lighthouses very quickly and efficiently.

'What's it like when you run into bad weather?' I asked Captain Davidson. 'Well, we were out at North Rona when a storm blew up suddenly from the north. Our anchor chain snapped. You just pin yourself into a corner and hope for the best... Then we ran with the swell, so it wasn't so bad... You just think about the pay packet at the end of the month.'

It was no surprise to learn that the two captains who

Opposite *The helicopter deck of the* Pharos
Below *Preparing material for the helicopter lift to Haskeir*
Bottom *The* Pharos' *galley steward, Bobby Fletcher*

share the *Pharos*, Captain Davidson and Captain Tulloch, are both Orcadians (though Captain Davidson has moved to North Connell) – Orkney has for centuries nurtured some of the best seafarers.

Captain Tulloch started his working life as an Ordinary Seaman on the *Pole Star* in 1970, and after marrying six years later, became First Mate on the *St Ola*, the ferry which crosses the Pentland Firth every day linking Stromness with Scrabster on Scotland's north coast. And then followed a return to the Northern Lights and eventually onto the new *Pharos*.

'My favourite is the west coast,' says Captain Tulloch, 'cruising around the Outer Hebrides in the summer, about Barra and Benbecula. It's as near to Heaven as you'll get.'

ISLE OF MAN

POINT OF AYRE

There were still palm trees growing in the former keepers' garden at the Point of Ayre, though they looked bit weather-beaten now. Fred Fox, the Attendant, was showing me around. An old car lay abandoned at the base of the tower. The old store building has been converted into a stand-by engine room, control room and battery room.

Fred is also Attendant to Maughold Head Lighthouse, on the north-east corner of Man

Above *Point of Ayre Lighthouse*
Below *Detail from Maughold Head Lighthouse*

Established	1818
Automated	1991
Engineer	Robert Stevenson
Character	Flashing 4 white every 20 sec
Range	19 miles

DOUGLAS HEAD

Douglas Head lighthouse

'Douglas Head is unique in many ways, quite apart from there being no road into the station. Every single item has to be carried in and out over a series of steps and paths, as the removal men who brought us from Scotland learned to their cost! It took from 9.00 am until 6.00 pm to move our effects in, and those of Mr Wilson out.' So read the Station Notes of the NLB Journal from the summer of 1982 as recorded by Alistair Henderson, ALK.

The original lens has been removed and now stands in the Manx National Heritage Museum.

Established	1857
Automated	1986
Engineer	David & Thomas Stevenson
Character	Flashing white every 10 sec
Range	24 miles

PORT ERIN & THOUSLA ROCK

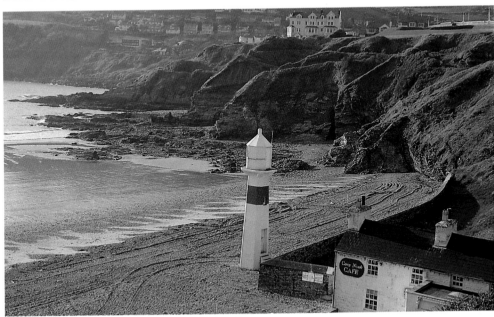

Left *Port Erin lighthouse*
Below *The memorial to shipwrecked crew of the 19th century French schooner,* Jeanne St Charles *on Thousla Rock*

High wind and torrential rain swept over the southern tip of the Isle of Man as I sat in the Sound Café wondering what to do next. I had come here to look at my next destination, the Calf of Man. There had been no boats to the Calf for days.

I read a leaflet about the Thousla Rock – a big wooden cross stood near the café car park overlooking Calf Sound.

The cross is a memorial to the wreck of a French schooner, the *Jeanne St Charles*, which was lost on Thousla Rock in 1858. The crew clung to the rock until the Port St Mary lifeboat arrived. But then, at the last minute, the two ship's boys lost their grip and were swept to their deaths in the swirling water. The lifeboat, meanwhile, with the rest of the crew, continued to Port Erin on the sheltered side of the island.

I drove over to Port Erin. Rows of tall, elegant houses lined the high land overlooking the harbour and the bay. I photographed the harbour light on the deserted beach, just below the tall houses.

Established	Not available
Automated	Built as automatic
Engineer	Not available
Character	Fixed red
Range	5 miles

CALF OF MAN

When there were keepers on the Calf, Juan Clague went to 'the rock' once a week in his boat from Port St Mary, weather permitting: one week to take the stores and papers, the next to do the reliefs.

'One keeper was so anxious to get off the island he climbed up my back as I was tying up the boat,' recalled Juan.

'During the Christmas and New Year reliefs, the keepers on the rock would radio to say that the weather was perfect for a boat-landing,' continued Juan… 'Then the keepers at the Shore-station would tell me the sea was too rough!'

There could be sheer farce – 'One time,' said Juan, 'there were no keepers waiting for the relief at the south landing. So I sailed around to the other landing on the other side of the island. But by then the keepers had gone over to the south landing. Since I saw no-one at my landing, I went straight back to the south landing. Well, this repeated itself once more until I stayed at the south landing, and I stayed put…'

I visited the Calf for one day. It had been three years since the new light had been automated. On my walk over the island, a pair of choughs, scarlet beaks and legs and delicate cries, wheeled over my head and landed in a field to probe for insects. Eleven pairs of choughs breed on the Calf, the highest concentration in Britain. There was even a pair nesting in the former PLK's sitting-room fireplace in the old High Light (one of the two lights which were abandoned in 1875).

Established	1968 (orig. 1818; discont. 1875)
Automated	1995
Engineer	P.H. Hyslop (1968 light)
Character	Flashing white every 15 sec
Range	26 miles

EAST COAST

ST ABB'S HEAD

Above *St Abb's lighthouse*

Below *the light*

This lighthouse is where I began my coastal journey for the first *At Scotland's Edge*. I stood at the first door I came to, and thought 'I've a few doors ahead of me', and knocked. And knocked again. Fortunately, I got off to a good start – I knew Jimmy Watt, the Assistant Keeper and his family, having met them earlier on Fair Isle. I'd also met Ernie England, another Assistant, and his family in Orkney before. The PLK showed me around. At the tower door, I started to take off my shoes before entering. 'This is not a temple, man!' he said.

But now, St Abb's Head Lighthouse was deserted, having been automated in 1993. Security fencing surrounds the tower and a notice at the gate stated:

> No Admittance
> PRIVATE
> KEEP OUT
> GUARD DOGS

Not quite deserted. I found a joiner working on one of the empty houses. He said he remembered coming here as a child – his father was a coastguard – and he used to play with the lighthouse children.

A fresh breeze swept up the cliffs. The air was filled with the heady mixture of guano and sea air. The ledges were crammed with guillemots and kittiwakes. A guide book claimed there were 60,000 seabirds, and eight different species, breeding here. It also told me: 'The Head is made of pink and purple lavas poured from volcanoes 400 million years ago. Holes can be seen in the cliffs where gas bubbles were trapped in the hardening lava.'

Established	1862
Automated	1993
Engineer	David & Thomas Stevenson
Character	Flashing white every 10 sec
Range	26 miles

BARN'S NESS

Above *Barns Ness lighthouse*

There was a traffic hold-up on the A1 near Barn's Ness – about three miles south of Dunbar. New dualling work had left huge mounds of red earth along the road-side. I glanced over to the coast – beyond the clutter of the main London to Edinburgh railway line. A little to the south stood the huge white and grey blocks of Torness Power Station. Just to the north – the dust of a cement works. Beyond the railway line, bulldozers worked over a huge landfill site with its attendant flock of gulls.

The little white tower of Barn's Ness Lighthouse stood near the top centre of ththis busy picture. I turned off the A1 near the power station, and followed the lane as far as the lighthouse gate.

A walled garden with curving lawn-edges and borders of orange and blue flowers lay in front of the neat white cottage. I knocked on the door…

In summer 1973 James Murray, the PLK wrote in the Lighthouse Journal of the lighthouse's popularity with visitors: 'In the last three months I have shown over the lighthouse on organised visits by schools, Boys' Brigades, Girl Guides – over 1,000 children.

'On one day alone I had 15 disabled people from North Berwick, 57 children from Cornbank School, 100 children from Mary Erskine School…

'At the time of writing this letter the telephone is still ringing with more camps wishing to visit the lighthouse.'

Established	1901
Automated	1986
Engineer	David A. Stevenson
Character	Isophase white every 4 sec
Range	10 miles

NORTHERN LIGHTHOUSE BOARD HEADQUARTERS

Simply referred to as '84' by generations of keepers after the number on the door, the Northern Lighthouse Board's headquarters stand on Edinburgh's broad, handsome, mile-long George Street. Built originally as part of the city's elegant 18th-century New Town development, '84' consisted of two grand flats, one upper and one lower. Later, as '84' needed more space, the town house next door, number 82, was acquired.

Now with a staff of over one hundred people, the three main departments of '84' are Engineering, Operations, and Finance and Administration, which maintain 200 lighthouses and 120 buoys around the coast of Scotland and the Isle of Man. For 1997–98, the annual running cost of the NLB will be over £17 million.

It is well over 20 years since I first walked up the steps into '84', then to attend an interview for the post of Roving Relief Lightkeeper. I walked out again an hour later with a passport to the Northern Lights, and with

Above *'84'*

Opposite top *Robert Stevenson, a major figure in the history of Scotland's lighthouses*

Opposite left *James Taylor, Chief Executive of the NLB*

Opposite right *Bob Watt, ex-keeper*

instructions to go first to the Bass Rock Lighthouse – via Leith Docks. The old *Pharos* anchored off the island, and I was lowered in the work-boat, winched up to the Bass landing in a basket, and joined the keepers in maintaining the paraffin light for a fortnight. It was mid-December. On three nights I cleared snow off the lantern after blizzards. Each afternoon the PLK, Dougie MacAffer, played his bagpipes in the engine room. Then followed a year around the coast – Mull of Kintyre, in deep snow; Sanda, a haunted, eerie place; Dunnet Head, and summer tourists; Pentland Skerries in spring, and a fall of migrant goldcrests; Sule Skerry, and the arrival of the first puffins; North Ronaldsay, and a remote island communi-ty... a string of magical names became reality.

From his spacious ground-floor office, the Board's Chief Executive, Captain James Taylor, keeps a keen eye over the organisation. Safe on terra firma now, after a career in the Royal Navy where he ultimately became Chief Staff Officer of the Submarine Flotilla, he gave me some of his thoughts on the future. The automation of

the last lighthouse was only weeks away: 'Too many peo-ple regard the automation process – and consequent removal of the lightkeepers – somehow as the closure of the Lighthouse Service. In fact nothing could be further from the truth... There is still the need, above all, to ensure the safety of the mariner at sea. Automation does not change that – it means we are providing the same service to at least as high a standard, but in a different way... a less romantic way, some would say, and on a calm and clear day, under a perfect blue sky at Hyskeir, they are probably right... ' With a streamlined, modern, auto-matic future, there is still a need for someone to keep an eye on the lights, locally.

Captain Taylor continued: 'The Attendants are the men and women who actually allow us to get the job done. They are the eyes and ears of the Northern Lighthouse Board in the local coastal community in just the same way as the full-time Lightkeepers always were... That link, I'm happy to say, will always be there... '

GRANTON DEPOT

I n its heyday, the Granton Depot bustled with life, overflowing with supplies for all the lighthouses and their keepers. Names of the lighthouses, on large enamel plates, lined the shelves. Vast supplies of paint, ropes, nails, brass-polish, brooms, flags… it all passed through the hands of the Granton Store team who organised and dispatched the orders.

While the light-keepers' orders have stopped coming, the engineers' orders have taken over. Today, tons of machinery and building materials bound for the lighthouses under modernisation programmes pass through the depot.

Above left *Gordon Wishart, Buoy Foreman*
Above right *Exterior wall plaque, Granton Depot*
Left *Old clocks removed from lighthouses after demanning and stored at Granton pending their sale at auction*

OXCARS

Left *Oxcars*
Below *Inside the lantern*

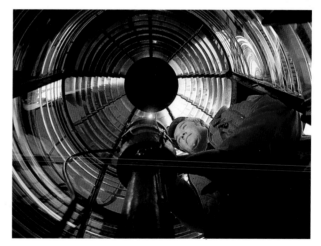

The Firth of Forth is fisherman Bill Simpson's patch. In the summer he fishes for crabs and lobsters along its shores, and in the winter catches what he calls 'snotty-buckies' (whelks). He uses a beautiful and sturdy 1910 Norwegian fishing boat which he salvaged from the bottom of the Firth a few years ago. Salvaging – that's another of Bill's jobs.

Bill took over as Attendant under tragic circumstances when his predecessor drowned just off the Oxcar light in 1981. And on Inchkeith's automation, he became Attendant there too.

Before sunrise in mid September, Bill and I left the jetty at Port Edgar, and crept in the gloom under the great girders and cantilevers of the Forth Railway Bridge. We passed a dainty little lighthouse protecting the southern support of the bridge, and crossed the Firth to land first on Inchcolm, near St. Comb's Abbey. After checking the light – just a lamp on top of a rod – we crossed the Firth again to visit Oxcars. Inside the tower, we climbed in the semi-darkness up to the lantern where Bill checked the gas and cleaned the windows. A little plaque beside the lens read: 'Dioptric Fixed Light Apparatus, 3rd Order, Designed by T & D Stevenson, Engineers. Barbiere and Finestre, Paris, and Dove & Co, Edinburgh, manufacturers, 1885'.

The Oxcars light was first lit on the night of 15th February 1886, but by 1894 it had become the first of the Northern Lights to be automated.

Established	1886
Automated	1894
Engineer	David & Thomas Stevenson
Character	Flashing 2 white/red every 7 sec
Range	White 13 miles, red 12 miles

INCHGARVIE

This little light first caught my eye as I was driving over the Forth Road Bridge. It is not one of the NLB lights, but is under the management of the Forth Ports Authority.

To take the photographs, I had to walk to the end of the breakwater which pushed into the estuary near Port Edgar. As the daylight faded and the wind dropped, I started photographing. The occasional train rumbled over the bridge.

I discovered later that the Inchgarvie Light sits on a brick pier, just about all that survives of the first attempt to build a railway bridge over the Forth in the 1870s.

The designer of this first attempt was Sir Thomas Bouch, who had already completed work on a railway bridge over the Tay estuary. But when the Tay bridge collapsed and a passenger train plunged into the water on the night of 28th December 1879, Bouch's world came to an abrupt end. His Forth Bridge contract was cancelled, and within a year the poor man had died of shock and despair.

The present Forth Rail Bridge was built during the 1880s by a four-man engineering team. During the construction, Bouch's old brick pier was topped with the Inchgarvie Light, leaving a sad memorial to a tragic life.

ELIE NESS

Left *Attendant Keeper Eddie Stephen*

Established	1929
Automated	1974
Engineer	David A. Stevenson
Character	Flashing white every 6 sec
Range	18 miles

A framed certificate hangs on the sitting-room wall of Eddie and Margaret Stephen's bungalow in the village of Elie: 'To Edward Stephen, Postman, Anstruther, for his dedication and commitment maintaining the Elie Ness Lighthouse over the past 20 years, which reflects great credit on him and Royal Mail, this 30th day of June 1995.'

Through the window, on the green of the crescent, oystercatchers probed the earth while gulls did their paddling trick to bring worms to the surface.

Eddie has been a postman since 1964, and became Attendant to the Elie light ten years later (his father was the Attendant before him).

It was late January when we visited the lighthouse. Eddie cycled, while I drove down to the dunes. A skein of over 200 greylag geese flew northwards beneath a pale watery sky as we walked over to Elie Ness.

FIFE NESS
THE NORTH CARR LIGHTSHIP

The North Carr Rocks have been a tricky problem for the NLB over the years. Early in the 19th century, the reef, which extends for a mile and a half from Fife Ness, was marked with a buoy. But the buoy broke free from its moorings five times. A stone beacon was designed a little later by Robert Stevenson, but it was destroyed by a storm just before its completion. So in 1821 a cast-iron beacon was built, and it still stands today.but the problem was not finally solved as the beacon did not carry a light.

A spare lightship was brought into service from Trinity House in 1887, and anchored off the notorious reef, and twelve years later replaced by a purpose-built vessel.

The third and final North Carr Lightship began its service in 1933. With a light and fog-horn, it warned shipping until 1975. However, even with this vessel, life was far from plain sailing. On 8th December 1959, the lightship, with her seven-man crew, broke her moorings in one of the worst east-coast storms in decades. The Broughty Ferry Lifeboat made an attempt to reach the drifting vessel but all nine of the lifeboat crew were lost when enormous waves swamped them (the lightship crew were eventually brought to safety in one of the first helicopter rescues in Scotland).

The North Carr Lightship is presently berthed at Dundee harbour, abandoned for the moment, after lying in Anstruther harbour where she had proved to be too costly to operate as a museum.

When the lightship was removed from the service off the North Carr in 1975, the new automatic Fife Ness Lighthouse was ready to take over. It is regularly checked today by Dave Whitehead, a Sector-Officer of the Coastguard, who lives next door.

Established	1975
Automated	Built as automatic
Engineer	P. H. Hyslop
Character	Iso white/red every 10 sec
Range	WhHite 21 miles/red 20 miles

Middle *Attendant dave whitehead in lantern*
Bottom *North Carr lightship*

TAYPORT LIGHTS
& BUDDON NESS

I looked through my binoculars at the Pile Light – an old wooden tower a few hundred yards off Tayport. It had been built to replace the two stone Tayport Lights – the High and the Low – in 1848 and had been abandoned as a lighthouse over forty years ago. Cormorants were now roosting on the dome and the balcony railings.

Someone on the pier called 'You should look for Charlie Gall', and pointed to his house across the harbour. 'His father was a Keeper on the Pile – the last one.' After explaining my interest, Charlie suggested we wait three hours and go in his boat to the Pile when the tide was right.

We made our way up the shaky steps of the Pile, and reached the door, jammed open with guano. In fact the guano half-filled the only room. But I could still see the beauty of the pine panelling, and the wooden bunks and cupboards. There was the top of a range only just visible, opposite the bunks, and a narrow ladder led up to the lantern. The loo was in a tiny shed below us, on the open deck just above the high water mark.

Top and bottom *The Pile Light, Tayport*
Centre *Tayport High and Low*

59

On the vast sand-dune peninsula of Barry Buddon, where the northern shores of the Firth of Tay meet the North Sea, stand two derelict lighthouses. Built in 1866 by Dundee's harbour authority, they were an attempt to mark and light this coast of constantly shifting sand-banks. But the coast was so changeable that by 1884, the lower of the two towers had to be moved intact 160 feet to a new position. The engineers took about a month to complete this extraordinary operation.

The two towers, however, became obsolete and were switched off. They are now within the Army's Barry Buddon Training Camp (the Army first took over the site in 1897), where around 30,000 men and women train every year with infantry weapons.

SCURDIE NESS

After visiting the lighthouse with the Attendant Keeper, Donald Cameron, I made my way along the north bank of the South Esk estuary opposite the village of Ferryden. The lights in the windows were coming on, one by one, in a row of waterside cottages. I photographed the tower in the still evening.

On the day when Scurdie Ness was lit for the first time, on Tuesday 1st March 1870, there were great celebrations in the village of Ferryden and in Montrose. Scores of boats in the harbour were adorned with colourful bunting, and excited crowds gathered on the estuary banks. Almost every window in Ferryden was illuminated. A huge procession assembled, at the lighthouse, of villagers, the Naval Reserve, the Volunteer Life Brigade, torch bearers and the village band, as they waited for the great moment.

Donald Cameron's great-grandfather would have been amongst the throng – he was coxswain of the Montrose lifeboat at the time. (Donald follows the family tradition, and is a crew member of the Tyne Class Lifeboat.)

Up in the lantern of the new lighthouse, on that March evening in 1870, the light-keepers prepared the paraffin apparatus and raised the roller blinds. Then, at precisely 6.00 pm, inside the fixed lens, the mantle was lit for the first time 'amid cheers from the multitude'.

A tugboat laden with sightseers sailed up and down the river, the town bells rang, and rockets were fired. Then the procession marched towards Ferryden where a huge bonfire was lit, before congregating in the Town Hall of Montrose for a great banquet. The speeches and toasts and revelry went on right through the night.

Established	1870
Automated	1987
Engineer	David & Thomas Stevenson
Character	Flashing 3 white every 20 sec
Range	23 miles

TOD HEAD

The day I arrived at Tod Head Lighthouse, someone was cutting the banister rails to make way for electricity cables and computer equipment. The noise from the metal-cutter screamed through the tower.

But up in the light-room, everything was still intact. The desk and chair, and the brass clock, and the barometer, they were all there. Three weeks later, everything was removed before more renovations, and delivered to Scotland's Lighthouse Museum. The Tod Head paraphernalia now forms the impressive Tod Head Room in the former sitting room of Kinnaird Head's Assistant Light-Keeper's cottage.

The last keeper at Tod Head was Magnus Pearson, who lived here with his wife Fiona. They met on the Rhinns of Islay when Magnus was a keeper there in the early 1960s and they married soon after. At one stage they lived on the Isle of May, when the lighthouse population reached eleven – including their own two children who were born there. 'It was a lovely place,' said Fiona, 'One hundred and forty acres in all – it wasn't a wee island.'

With Tod Head's automation in 1988, Magnus became a Travelling PLK. He had a month at Pladda, and was later posted to the Bass Rock. But on his second spell at the Bass, Magnus had a massive heart attack, and he died there. 'I had twenty happy years with Magnus… not long enough, but it was a very happy time,' said Fiona.

Following Magnus's death, Fiona wrote a moving letter to the NLB Journal (Christmas 1988) from Tod Head: 'We had a service at the Church of Lunna across the Vidlin Voe from Magnus's family home…I miss Magnus, my husband for 20 years, so very much, but am comforted to know that he died with friends doing what he liked best to do. Being a good lighthouse keeper.'

Established	1897
Automated	1988
Engineer	David A. Stevenson
Character	Flashing 4 white every 30 sec
Range	29 miles

Above *Tod Head lightroom*
Below *Attendant Keeper Douglas Stevenson*

BUCHAN NESS

The acre of lighthouse ground takes up the whole of the island of Buchan Ness but linked as it is to the village of Boddam with a little footbridge, this is one of the least isolated of the Scottish lights.

Bob Duthie retired as PLK at Buchan Ness in 1988, after nearly forty years with his wife in the service. They were at Buchan Ness early in Bob's career, too; their daughter often got a soaking when she dashed over the footbridge on a winter's morning to catch the bus to school.

'End fog-horn torment – plea' ran a *Dundee Courier* headline on 25th March 1996. The Buchan Ness lighthouse fog-horn had been disturbing the residents of Boddam, the village 300 metres across the water, for ninety years.

'In thick weather,' continued the report, 'they can have three mind-numbing blasts every minute for five days.' But things came to a head with the tragic news of a young boy, suffering from leukaemia, who lives in Boddam. He needed peace and quiet to rest after his fortnightly treatment – and so came the request for switching the fog-horn off.

'Complaints have never produced any action,' the *Courier* reported, though the boy's grandfather believed that all 2,500 people of the village, including the fishermen, wanted the horn switched off.

Bob Duthie, retired Attendant (and once stationed at this light), occasionally calls on an old pal in Boddam, and they walk over the footbridge to Buchan Ness. Now that the lighthouse is automatic and the keepers' quarters are sold to a private owner, they walk around the lighthouse wall to take in the sea air.

Above *Attendant Gordon Stewart*
Below *Bob Duthie and his wife, retired from Buchan Ness*

Established	1827
Automated	1988
Engineer	Robert Stevenson
Character	Flashing white every 5 seconds
Range	28 miles

RATTRAY HEAD

Above *Gordon Stewart and John Buchan*

Gordon Stewart is the tractor-man to Rattray Head. Once a fortnight, he drives over the sands to the lighthouse with the Attendant, John Buchan, a hardy type of 80 years.

John Buchan was a deep-sea fisherman all his working life, around the waters of the Faroes, Iceland and Rockall. On retirement, he needed something just a bit different to do, and when he heard about the Rattray job from a Customs Officer, he offered his service to '84'. So, since the age of 65, he has made the fortnightly trip over the sands at low tide – and in winter the trip is often in darkness in order to coincide with low tide.

At the tower, John and Gordon climb the 32-foot vertical ladder on the outside before reaching the door to the first floor where the generators and batteries are housed.

The Rattray tower is only half a mile as the crow flies from the Shore Station just beyond the beach and the dunes. Before a phone was installed, Keeper Bob Shand used to communicate by semaphore from the lighthouse to his wife, who had a clear view from their bedroom window.

But the first phone at Rattray was installed by some enterprising keepers who rigged up telephone wires from the top of the lighthouse to a sturdy pole in the dunes near the Shore Station, a half-mile stretch. This worked well for a few years, and only ended when a Shackleton aircraft, flying low and following the coast, hit and snapped the wires in 1957.

Established	1895
Automated	1982
Engineer	David A. Stevenson
Character	Flashing 3 white every 30 sec
Range	24 miles

KINNAIRD HEAD

When Jim Oliver, the Assistant Manager of Scotland's Lighthouse Museum, busies himself around the magnificent collection of old lenses and paraphernalia which has found a final resting place at Kinnaird Head, he doesn't suffer from melancholy over a lost way of life. As an ex-PLK, he has been stationed at many of Scotland's major lights, and instead sees the museum as a dynamic way forward, and he revels in its success with the general public and his ex-light-keeping colleagues.

'Jim passes on his feelings as well as his knowledge about lighthouse life' said Richard Townsley, the museum's manager. 'We're still very close to what the objects in the museum were used for, and even the rest of the staff feel close to the NLB too.'

Moving from Worcester Museums to the new museum in Fraserburgh, Richard was very soon under the spell of the 'Northern Lights'. 'You can't help getting wrapped up in it', he told me. 'I've met keepers, boatmen and tractor-drivers, crawled over rocks and climbed remote towers… It's fascinating work.'

The museum's main entrance hall houses a stunning collection of lighthouse lenses, four from major lights and six from minor lights. I gasped at the beauty of some of them, their perfect prisms and rainbow colours.

'We're here to portray the history of the lighthouse service in Scotland,' said Richard, 'and we see ourselves as inheritors of the NLB traditions, to keep alive what it was like to be in the wide family of light-keeping.'

At the door of the old Kinnaird Head Lighthouse, Richard enthused about the tower. 'Our guides show visitors around a real lighthouse, which was left exactly as it was when it became redundant. You can't do that at other stations now. And the new automatic light nearby sits alongside the old technology. We have a special situation here.'

The new light stands just below the old Kinnaird Castle tower. It is all-electric, and simply a small tower surrounded by a wooden fence. Most visitors would hardly notice it. But in its own way, it is just as remarkable as any of the old lights.

So I was fascinated to read an article someone had submitted to the *Lighthouse Journal* recounting the first years of the NLB:

Jim Oliver of Scotland's Lighthouse Museum

After a season of bad storms and shipwrecks in 1782, the clamour for lights around the Scottish coast produced both the Board, in 1786, and its first lighthouse at Kinnaird, in 1787. It was there that the Board's first engineer, Thomas Smith, cut his teeth on lighthouse construction, and where their first keeper, a retired sea captain called James Park, was employed at a shilling a night.

The light was rebuilt by Smith's son-in-law, Robert Stevenson, modernised by his son, Alan Stevenson and modernised again by his grandson, David A. Stevenson, with a new lens in 1902.

Established	1787
Automated	1991
Engineer	Thomas Smith
Character	Flashing white every 5 seconds
Range	22 miles

Above *Lighthouse lens on display in the museum*

Bottom *Tour guides Alex Harrison and Sandy Taylor*

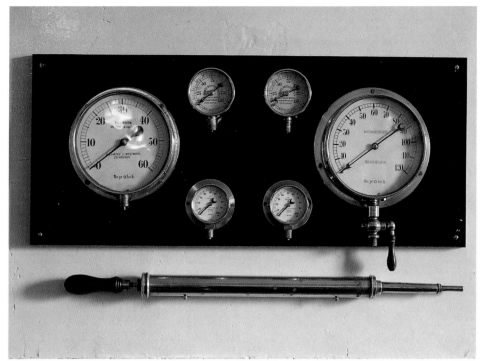

Above *Instrumentation in the fog-horn engine room*

Below *A school party at the museum*

COVESEA SKERRIES

Above *Alex Campbell*

I climbed the tall Covesea tower with Attendant Keeper Alex Campbell. On the balcony, he told me of his life as a fisherman. Occasionally, pairs of Tornado Fighters from nearby RAF Lossiemouth roared off the runway.

'I just loved being a fisherman, it was my whole life,' he said. 'I fished for thirty years in a Seine Netter from the Norwegian sector to Rockall.' He's a religious man – a deacon in the local Baptist Church – and he decided to give up the fishing to see more of his family.

Alex misses the boat and the sea very much. Even having experienced the boat going down 'under a huge lump of water' when he was in the wheelhouse… 'I'll never understand how we came up again.'

Looking east from the balcony, the Silver Sands Caravan Park is Covesea's nearest neighbour. (This part of Scotland is very tame.) Beyond are the Old and New Murray Golf Courses. Looking west, there is a small tower above the beach – a look-out post run by pupils of Gordonstoun School – and beyond, fields and woods,

and the wide yellow sands of Lossiemouth Bay.

The two former keepers' cottages at Covesea are now holiday accommodation for use by anyone connected with the lighthouse service. Even light-keepers come here, for a real busman's holiday.

Alex is now the Caretaker of the cottages, as well as the Attendant Light-Keeper; and since leaving the sea, he has became a milkman in Lossiemouth.

Established	1846
Automated	1984
Engineer	Alan Stevenson
Character	Flashing white/red every 20 sec
Range	White 24 miles, red 20 miles

CRAIGTON

The Kessock Bridge spans the narrows between the Beauly and the Moray Firths, just north of Inverness. It's an elegant suspension bridge, and its north end almost stands over the Craigton Lighthouse.

I drove over the bridge and turned off the main road to pass a series of smart new bungalows, all pebbledash, little lawns and rockeries. Leslie and Beth Munro arrived soon after me, to check over the light. Beth is the Attendant – her father and grandfather were light-keepers in the Northern Lights, and she was keen to keep up the family connection – though she lives now with her family in Oldtown Road, on a housing estate on the other side of Inverness.

Above Craigton and Kessock Bridge

Established	1904
Automated	Built as automatic
Engineer	David A. Stevenson
Character	Flashing wht/red/grn every 4 sec
Range	White 11/red 7/green 7 miles

CHANONRY & CROMARTY

In fading daylight, I set my camera and tripod on Chanonry Point's shingle beach. Small groups of people began to gather near me, silently waiting to watch bottle-nosed dolphins in the Firth. The light switched on at the lighthouse.

For the last four years, the Attendant Keeper has been Anne MacEachren, who took on the job from her husband Archie when he became too infirm to climb the lighthouse stairs. Archie was in the lighthouse service for sixty-five years, having started off as an Ordinary Seaman as a lad on the *Pharos*.

He later became a light-keeper, which included a stint at Chanonry, a one-man station by that time. It was while he was here that he met Anne, who lived nearby.

Archie was born at St Abb's Head Lighthouse where his father was a light-keeper too. Now his wife has become an Attendant Keeper. 'We like to keep it in the family,' said Anne. She is also Chanonry's Observer, as the light is visible from their Rosemarkie house.

The original optics of Chanonry Lighthouse were removed in 1984, being replaced with a biform optic, and have been put on display in the porch of Fortrose Academy.

Below *Cromarty lighthouse*
Bottom right *Douglas Matheson, Cromarty Lighthouse*

Above *Chanonry*

Cromarty

The two former keepers' cottages by Cromarty Lighthouse are now used by Aberdeen University's Dolphin and Seal Research Establishment, while the tower continues to be maintained by Douglas Matheson, the Attendant Keeper since automation in 1985. He lives about 50 yards down the road from the light, and can see it shining each night from his bedroom.

Douglas was an Occasional Keeper before the light was automated. He was also the Auxiliary in Charge of the Cromarty Coastguard – in the days when they practised with rockets and breeches buoy.

He knew the keepers and their families at the lighthouse in his childhood in the 1920s, and he remembers their gardens overflowing with vegetables. The keepers sold much of their produce to the Cromarty folk.

The last keeper was John Harrow – when the light was already a one-man station. He was given a grand 'do' on the *Pharos*, which anchored off-shore in the Firth. In earlier days, the *Pharos* would arrive to fill two enormous tanks at the lighthouse with acetylene. But by the 1930s, electricity came to the town, and the lighthouse was electrified at the same time.

CLYTHNESS

I found David Nicholson harrowing a small field near Clythness, in preparation for a crop of oats. He is the Attendant Keeper to the Clythness Light, having taken over from his father in 1980. David's father took over on his father's retirement as Occasional Keeper.

David stopped his tractor on my approach. The seagulls which had been following him flew off for a while. He runs about 180 acres of grain, sheep and cattle on these fertile well-drained Caithness slopes. He kindly agreed to meet me at the lighthouse an hour before sunset.

As the daylight began to fade, the charm of Clythness emerged slowly – the tower light beamed, and David stepped onto the balcony. The cottage looked neat in its white coat and green corner stones, and the sea and the sky became an eerie blue-grey blanket back-drop.

Established	1916
Automated	1964
Engineer	David A. Stevenson
Character	Flashing 2 white every 30 sec
Range	16 miles

NOSS HEAD

Above John Ross, Attendant Keeper in Noss Head control room

One of the saddest days on my lighthouse journey for this book was the day I visited Noss Head Lighthouse, a couple of miles north of Wick. I had spent three weeks at Noss as a Roving Keeper in 1975, when three families were living here. Sam Neighbour, the other Rover, had his lorry-home 'plugged-in' at Noss at the time. The place buzzed with life.

The shock came when I stood at the lighthouse gate. There was a coldness about the place. Some sheep ran out of the grounds. The tall, cast iron sundial plinth, once so lovingly painted, had been knocked over and cracked. I walked past the boarded-up engine room. I had seen enough abandoned engine rooms, and I felt sick with the memory of their copper and brass beauty, and their unique smell – a mixture of diesel and paraffin, and wax and paint.

I turned to the courtyard. The Keepers' cottages were completely derelict and all the windows had been smashed. Looking inside, I saw that the vandals had been thorough.

I met crofter-fisherman John Ross, the Attendant Keeper, and he told me the story. The buildings, except the immaculate tower, had been sold to an Arab who had never visited the place in ten years.

Noss was a paraffin light when I was a Keeper here. It was always a pleasure to light up – to pre-heat the paraffin-pipe for a few minutes with a meths burner, while raising each of the roller-blinds around the lantern. Then I'd release the winding-brake and gently push-start the revolving optics. By then, it was ready to light up – I'd turn on the gas and put a burning taper to the silk mantle. There'd be a momentary 'floop' as the flame took, and the place was alive for the night.

Established	1849
Automated	1987
Engineer	Alan Stevenson
Character	Flashing white/red every 20 sec
Range	White 25 miles, red 21 miles

NORTH COAST

CAPE WRATH

&LOCH ERIBOLL

Cape Wrath is Britain's 'Empty Quarter', as Paul Theroux called it in his book about Britain and the British, *The Kingdom by the Sea*. I looked at the O.S. map of the area before going over. 'Danger Area' was written eight times across the peninsula. A small group of people had gathered near a boat-landing on the shores of the Kyle of Durness. A Canadian couple in the group told me about their house by Lake Ontario (with a photo-album to prove it) which they have designed to look like an authentic Canadian lighthouse – a square, wooden tower with adjoining living quarters, and even with a lantern housing a Fresnel lens which they illuminate on special occasions.

After the Navy had stopped shelling a Cape Wrath hillside from three warships off the north coast, we were able to cross the Kyle and head for the lighthouse. (Two Mercedes mini-buses were waiting to take us along the 11 mile track.)

At the lighthouse, Ron Nixon, an Assistant Keeper, was repairing what was obviously a poacher's salmon net in the courtyard. 'It's a badminton net,' he tells me. 'We're all very keen on badminton out here!'

The PLK at the Cape is Jimmock Mackay. He's been in the headlines once or twice in his time. The most dramatic incident he was involved in was the Bell Rock Lighthouse fire in 1987, when a leaking diesel pipe caused devastation. All three keepers were able to run down the tower below the fire to the door, where they climbed the external ladder to the rocks – luck was on their side as the tide was out.

Another keeper at the Cape, Donny MacIver (a Relieving Keeper, out for a month) was caught out

Top Jimmock Mackay,
Cape Wrath control room
Centre Jimmock Mackay,
PLK, Ron Nixon and Alex
Smith, Assistant Keepers
Bottom Sundial

Cape Wrath

Established	1828
Automated	1998
Engineer	Robert Stevenson
Character	Flashing 4 white every 30 sec
Range	24 miles

Top *Loch Eriboll lighthouse*
Centre *Ken Black, AK*
Bottom *Donny MacIver and
Ron Nixon, Cape Wrath*

in a snow storm on Christmas Eve, 1995. He'd
gone down the road to collect the Christmas
mail, but a blizzard blew up and forced his
Landrover into a ditch. So Donny walked the
seven miles to an MOD bothy where there was
a telephone and a few Army rations. After
phoning for help, he bedded down for the night,
and in the morning a rescue helicopter picked
him up and delivered him back to the lighthouse.

As it had been Donny's turn to prepare the
Christmas lunch, the two Assistant Keepers
were glad to see him back. By 2.00 pm, the
table was set and the turkey with all the
trimmings was ready. The Cape Wrath three sat
down but just before carving, Donny took a
bottle into his hand and heaved a heavy sigh,
and said rather quietly, 'I think I'll start with just
a wee dram…'

Loch Eriboll

Established	1937
Automated	Built as automatic
Engineer	David A. Stevenson
Character	Flashing white/red every 3 sec
Range	White 13 miles, red 12 miles

STRATHY POINT

The huge white buildings of the Strathy Point Lighthouse seemed to hang mysteriously in great veils of mist in the summer heat as I drove towards it. I stopped by a small loch near the lighthouse, to bathe in the warm shallow water, crystal clear, over pure, white sand.

I met Tommy Eunson and his wife at the lighthouse. Tommy's retirement was just about to coincide with the light's automation, in early 1997. He started as an Occasional in the service, at Sumburgh Head in Shetland. Then a girl he was engaged to persuaded him to apply to the Northern Lights (he was a crofter at the time).

But soon after Tommy became a Supernumerary, his fiancée died, and he was stationed to his home islands, Shetland. It was during his appointment to Muckle Flugga Lighthouse that he met his wife, Barbara – in the Haroldswick Stores, on Unst.

'It suits us here at Strathy,' said Barbara. 'We're out on a limb, but that's how we like it. We're both from "out on a limb" – I came from the north end of Shetland, while Tommy came from the south end.'

Established	1958
Automated	1997
Engineer	P. H. Hyslop
Character	Flashing white every 20 sec
Range	27 miles

When Strathy Point Lighthouse was lit for the first time on 1st May, 1958, the beam of 600,000 candle power was the most powerful of all the Northern Lights.

Bob Duthie is a retired keeper now living near Buchan Ness Lighthouse. He is the only surviving member of Strathy Point's first three light-keepers: 'It was all right at Strathy, oh aye, no complaints there. Our boy got a taxi every day to the school, so that was handy.' His wife was thrilled with the all-electric house, having moved with Bob from Sanda, a remote and primitive station off the Kintyre peninsula.

'We practised putting the light on during the day at Strathy,' said Bob. The three keepers were stationed there a month before the opening ceremony. 'Then we'd switch it off before sunset. Unique… !' said Bob.

The Commissioners came to Strathy Point for the official lighting ceremony. The top brass from '84' were there, as well as representatives from Trinity House and the Irish Lights.

The NLB's Senior Commissioner, Sir Robert Maconochie, performed the ceremonies. He pulled a switch in the light-room to officially light up for the first time, and in the fog-signal engine room he started the engines. In his speech he suggested that Strathy could be the last major lighthouse to be built in Scotland, and that he couldn't imagine that 'mechanism' would ever replace the reliability of light-keepers.

The Lord Lieutenant of Sutherland, Brigadier G.S. Rawstorne, made an attempt at a speech, but the fog-horn, interrupting him every forty-five seconds with four long blasts, succeeded in adding 'a touch of informality' to the proceedings.

Below (L toR) Dave Noble, Assistant Keeper; Tommy Eunson, PLK, and Barbara Eunson; Clive Babiak, Local Assistant Keeper

DUNNET HEAD

I drove to John O' Groats harbour to meet Bobby Dundas, the Attendant to Dunnet Head Lighthouse. As I waited for Bobby – he was still hauling lobster creels – I was entertained by the tourists.

A photographer with a tiny booth took photographs of an Australian couple standing beside a signpost which read 'PERTH 9524M'. When the photographer had finished, then the couple placed a large gnome below the sign-post and pointed a camcorder at it.

Then two elderly ladies walked up to the signpost, one to photograph the other with their own cameras, while the photographer tried to explain to them that this was his special site.

After about half an hour, Bobby arrived in the harbour, and we were soon on our way to Dunnet Head. The lighthouse stands on Britain's most northerly mainland point. I stayed in the bothy near the tower when I was a Roving Keeper; for three weeks I was Britain's most northerly mainland inhabitant, just a few yards further north than the three families who lived here then.

One of my fondest memories is of Johnny Sinclair, an old man of around 80 years of age, who came from Dunnet village once a week to take anyone who needed a lift into Thurso, for a shopping trip. Johnny drove a wonderful 1950s ex-London taxi, an Austin 8, and he always wore a dark pinstripe suit with wide lapels, and a trilby tilted to one side.

My only uncomfortable memory of my time during the happy weeks at Dunnet Head were the three days of fog, and three days of the fog-horn – three blasts every ninety seconds.

Established	1831
Automated	1989
Engineer	Robert Stevenson
Character	Flashing 4 white every 30 sec
Range	23 miles

Right *Bobby Dundas*

STROMA

I took this photograph from the balcony of Duncansby Head Lighthouse. The view looks north-west across Stroma and the Stroma light, and the Pentland Firth to Hoy, Orkney's high island.

This was the nearest I got to Stroma on this journey. But when I took the photograph, some of the technicians from '84' were working out there for a few days. One of them was Eddie Dishon. He happens to have a close connection with the island, and takes part in the annual 'Stroma Gathering'.

'It's a reunion of around a hundred people,' says Eddie. 'They're mostly former inhabitants of Stroma, including the light-keepers. The gathering is held at John O' Groats, and Jimmy Simpson, the 'Laird of Stroma', is usually MC. He can tell a tale or two, and we have a dinner-dance.'

'The veil of reality was always very thin in Stroma. Well, it was a strange place,' says Alistair McDonald. He had been a keeper there in the 1980s. 'With all the houses empty, it was a ghost island,' he continued.

'The keepers referred to the time of day on the island as Stroma-time. One hour would usually mean four hours.'

Alistair was on the 2–6 watch, the morning of 13th February 1997, when he received a phone call from the coastguard. It was 4.00 am. 'How are you?' enquired the coastguard. 'Oh, I'm fine, how's yourself?' replied Alistair, at the same time puzzled by the polite words. 'Well, I'm glad you're awake because you've got a ship on the rocks,' replied the coastguard.

The ship was the 13,000 ton Danish cargo vessel *Bettina Danica*, which had struck Stroma well out of sight of the lighthouse.

Alistair ran to the keepers' quarters: 'Kenny, we've a problem! We've got a ship on the rocks!'

Kenny replied, 'That's fine, put the kettle on!' The other keeper was wakened: 'I'll be right there!' In fact, all three keepers were 'right there', and gave the coastguard the ship's exact position. The Thurso lifeboat was soon on the scene, and took all the crew safely off. Three days later, the ship was a write-off.

View from Duncansby Head to Stroma

Established	1896
Automated	1996
Engineer	David A. Stevenson
Character	Flashing 2 white every 20 sec
Range	26 miles

DUNCANSBY HEAD

I reached Duncansby Head on a bright, windy summer's afternoon. The car park near the lighthouse was lined with tourists' cars. I met Bruce Brown, the PLK, and he gave me the use of the local assistant's quarters, now abandoned, to stay in.

The lighthouse stands in Scotland's extreme north-east mainland corner, and it was from here, until recently, that radio-contact was kept with the Rock Stations in the area. This contact, 'the speak', was made three times a day with Stroma, Pentland Skerries, Copinsay and Sule Skerry. (And once a day, 'the speak' was made to North Ronaldsay, a family station on the northernmost island of Orkney.)

Otherwise, the Duncansby Keeper on duty would act as switchboard operator, usually between the keepers and their wives, or phone calls from '84'. The conversations could be very one-sided when a keeper's wife was phoning, the wife being very chatty and sometimes personal, while the keeper would be very quiet or monosyllabic as he was very aware that their words were being broadcast through the loudspeakers of most of the lights in the north of Scotland.

As we sat on the newly-mown lighthouse lawn – the tower behind us, and the cliff-top in front – Bruce Brown told me of his life in the Service. (The wind had dropped, and we could hear the constant flapping of wings from great rafts of guillemots, bathing and preening, two hundred feet below us.)

Bruce started in the service in August 1959. He left his job as an electrician in Lochgelly, a Fife mining town, after hearing about the lighthouse

Established	1924
Automated	1997
Engineer	David A. Stevenson
Character	Flashing white every 12 sec
Range	24 miles

life from his cousin, who was already a keeper. 'Before I came into the Northern Lights,' said Bruce, 'the nearest I got to the sea was going along the prom in Kirkcaldy on a shopping trip with the wife!'

As a Supernumerary, Bruce's first six months were spent at lighthouses as diverse as Kinnaird Head, the tower in the town, and Hyskeir, the remote reef west of Rhum. His life since then has been a series of more or less five year stints at Ardnamurchan, Buchan Ness, Skerryvore, Killantringan, Bass Rock, Maughold Head and finally, Duncansby Head.

On Skerryvore during Bruce's time, the duty period was six weeks 'on the rock' alternating with three weeks ashore. 'The worst thing at Skerryvore,' said Bruce, 'was to see the ship arrive on relief day – I'd have my uniform on, my boots polished, and all my bags packed – and

then discover that the sea was too rough for the relief, and the next thing you'd see was the stern of the ship as she steamed back to Oban!'

'I nearly lost my life at Skerryvore,' said Bruce. 'I was washed off the grating by a huge wave during the relief. I was hauled out of the water, and I said to the other keeper – don't tell Hazel. (Bruce's wife). So we got back to Oban, and the first thing he did when we got to the Shore Station was to run up the stairs, knock on my door and shout "Hazel! Hazel! Bruce has been washed into the sea – at Skerryvore!"'

'I'll miss the light at Duncansby,' said Bruce. 'When I retire, and the light is automated, we're going to live in John O' Groats. I'll be able to look out of the back door and see the light shining.'

Right *Dave MacIlwrath, Assistant Keeper, and Bruce Brown, PLK*

ORKNEY

TORNESS

Attendant Keeper Hugh Seatter

Farmer Hugh Seatter has been the Attendant Keeper to the Torness light since November 1950. His home is well over a mile from the light, and these days he rides there on his Honda four-wheel-drive motorbike.

When he first took on the job, he had to walk – about once every four days to make acetylene gas at the tower to keep the light running. Later on, Hugh was supplied with gas cylinders; and the latest development has been the installation of solar panels to supply the light with electricity.

During the 1920s and 30s, several trawlers struck the rocks below Torness, before the light was built (it was first lit in 1937). The boats, from the east coast ports, mainly Aberdeen and Hull, had successfully navigated the treacherous waters of the Pentland Firth – where all the headlands and islands were well lit. Probably with relief the trawler-men emerged from the Firth to start the great crossing to the Faroes and Iceland – only to strike the nasty little point, Torness, which juts out of Hoy's southern, dark flank.

Established	1937
Automated	Built as automatic
Engineer	David A. Stevenson
Character	Flashing white every 3 seconds
Range	10 miles

CANTICK HEAD

The tower lights a key position where the entrance to Scapa Flow's sheltered waters meets the notorious Pentland Firth. It is through this narrow channel, dangerous with numerous reefs and islands, that all the shipping passes, to and from Orkney's French-owned oil terminal on Flotta (the 'flat island').

Two billion barrels of crude oil, processed on Flotta, have been carried by tanker through Cantick waters since the terminal was opened in 1977.

I stayed in the former Customs House at Lyness for three nights while I visited the Hoy lights. This part of the island is littered with a great variety of military buildings which have survived since the First and Second World Wars. Nissen huts have become tractor sheds, and there is even a former cinema foyer which has become a house.

Established	1858
Automated	1991
Engineer	David & Thomas Stevenson
Character	Flashing white every 20 sec
Range	18 miles

RUFF REEF

About a hundred arctic and common terns were roosting on the rocks at low tide, below the great iron legs of the Ruff Reef light. Periodically, the birds would rise together, and then spread out in a clamouring crowd, and silently settle to roost and preen again on the rocks.

Just beyond the light and the reef lies the island of Switha, uninhabited except for seals and storm petrels. And beyond Switha, the Sound of Hoxa and the Hoxa minor light, and to the north, the bright flame of the 'Flotta flare' at the oil terminal.

Established	1881
Automated	Built as automatic
Engineer	Thomas Stevenson
Character	Flashing 2 white every 10 sec
Range	6 miles

HOXA HEAD

Above *Hoxa Head overlooking Scapa Flow*

The 1900 Hoxa Head Lighthouse, cast-iron and gas-powered, must have been one of the smartest and most cared for in the service (which is saying something.) James Deerness, the Attendant, even stopped one of the Board's engineers from fixing a 'Standard' padlock to the tower door.

I photographed James and his father in August 1996 on the lighthouse balcony – and two months later I discovered that the tower had been dismantled and delivered to Scotland's Lighthouse Museum, and replaced by a glass-fibre kit lighthouse.

On Hoxa Head, near the light, are the remains of the 'Balfour Battery' – a collection of Second World War buildings which housed an observation tower and gun-emplacements once guarding this major entrance to Scapa Flow.

Established	1900
Automated	Built as automatic
Engineer	David A. Stevenson
Character	Flashing white/red every 3 sec
Range	White 9 miles, red 6 miles

Above *Hoxa Head light*
Below *James Deerness junior, Attendant Keeper, and his father,*
James senior, a previous Attendant Keeper

ROSENESS

I met the Attendant Keeper, John Smith, at his farm, Lower Cornquoy, in Holm, near the Churchill Barriers. 'We'll go in my car to the light,' he said, 'and then there won't be a problem walking the last bit. The folk at the road-end don't like people walking on their land except me.'

The tower is one of the most modern in Scotland, and stands only a hundred metres or so from a grand and sturdy 19th-century day mark – a conical stone base supporting a large wooden cross.

The original Roseness tower, a typical cast-iron minor light with a neat set of optics, now stands on display at Scotland's Lighthouse Museum. The tower served as the last chance for an accurate bearing by Commander Prien of the German U-boat, U47, as he crept into the heart of Scapa Flow on the night of 13th–14th October 1939 to torpedo the British battle-ship, *Royal Oak*. Eight hundred and thirty-three men lost their lives that night, while the submarine escaped back into the North Sea without being detected.

It was following the *Royal Oak* disaster that Winston Churchill ordered the construction of the barriers between some of Orkney's South Isles to block four potential entries into Scapa Flow.

Above *Attendant Keeper John Smith*

Established	1904
Automated	Built as automatic
Engineer	David A. Stevenson
Character	Flashing white every 6 seconds
Range	8 miles

COPINSAY

I joined Sidney Foubister, Copinsay's Attendant Keeper, on one of his fortnightly boat-trips over Deerness Bay to the lighthouse. His two young daughters and his father came too. It was over twenty years since I first set foot on the island as an RSPB summer warden, when I stayed in the abandoned farmhouse.

My only neighbours were the three keepers at the lighthouse – at the opposite side of the island, perched on the edge of a 200 feet high cliff. I'd often call in on the keepers, and it was there that I discovered the magic of a lighthouse – the huge, magnificent optics, a series of five dinner plate-sized lenses amongst a multitude of sparkling prisms all set in bronze, and the original 1915 paraffin lighting apparatus; and in the light-room, an oak desk and a chair, and the winding mechanism, which needed winding like a huge grand-father clock mechanism (every 45 minutes) through the night.

Each night, there was music in the light-room – from the hiss of the paraffin light, from the optics as it gently revolved, creaking eerily, and from the slow ping, ping, ping of a small brass plate which dropped onto each cog of one of the winding wheels.

In early summer, there was the background chorus from the sea-bird city on the cliff-ledges below the tower – a multitude of kittiwakes, guillemots and fulmars. And in midwinter, the rumble of the North Sea breakers pounded a deep rhythm in the darkness far below, while the wind moaned through the light-room's twelve bronze ventilators.

But now Copinsay was deserted. I didn't enjoy the visit – the heart of the place had been ripped out.

Established	1915
Automated	1991
Engineer	David A. Stevenson
Character	Flashing 5 white every 20 sec
Range	21 miles

HOY SOUND

These two lights, correctly called Hoy Sound (High) and Hoy Sound (Low), serve as leading lights for shipping entering Hoy Sound, the western gateway to Stromness and Scapa Flow. The lighthouses stand on Graemsay, the small island of around half a dozen farms and crofts, tucked between Hoy and Stromness.

In 1990, I lived in Stromness, working on the book *Sea Haven – Stromness in the Orkney Islands*. During the summer months, once a week, I took small groups of tourists to Graemsay for the day. My advertising literature included 'follow in the footsteps of Robert Louis Stevenson' – and so we did, to admire the beautifully made, but redundant, old pier, to walk along the white beach with its patches of coral sand, and down the track to Hoy Low where R.L.S. had his photograph taken in the 1880s,

standing in the lighthouse courtyard with his father, who was Engineer to the Board at the time.

After almost 20 years as a full-time Keeper at a string of major lights, Tommy Thompson gave it up to settle on Graemsay as a crofter and Attendant to Hoy High and Hoy Low leading lights whose towers stand over a mile apart.

I took some portraits of Tommy in the Hoy Low lantern for *At Scotland's Edge*, but since then he has moved off the island to live on the Orkney mainland following the death of his wife. He can check the lights from a high road above his house over 7 miles away and he still attends Hoy High and Hoy Low every Monday when he takes his boat over from Stromness.

Opposite *Hoy High*
Bottom *Hoy Low*

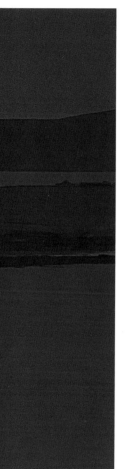

Hoy Low

Established	1851
Automated	1966
Engineer	Alan Stevenson
Character	Isophase white every 3 sec
Range	15 miles

Hoy High

Established	1851
Automated	1978
Engineer	Alan Stevenson
Character	Occulting white/red every 8 sec
Range	White 20 miles, red 16 miles

STROMNESS DEPOT

The Lighthouse Board's north of Scotland base is in Stromness, where there is a pier, office and workshops, and the Depot Manager's grand house. The *Fingal* is now based at the Depot, having replaced the *Pole Star*, following economy measures in 1995. (The *Pole Star* was sold to an American holiday company after more than three decades working around the Scottish coast and now sails the warm, blue waters off Florida.)

During my visit to Stromness for this book, six people, including the manager, were employed here. Most of their work was involved with buoy-maintenance, and the fortnightly helicopter reliefs to the last manned Rock Stations in the area, Cape Wrath and Fair Isle South.

It was from Stromness that I was flown by helicopter to Sule Skerry, thirty-five miles west of Orkney, when I was a Local Assistant Keeper. The flight usually took about twenty minutes. But there was one memorable exception when we flew out into a fierce westerly gale. The pilot was flying without a navigator, and he couldn't find the lighthouse. I was feeling very ill with air-sickness from the buffeting the helicopter was taking, when the pilot turned to me for help in spotting Sule Skerry. After about forty minutes into the journey, we were just about to turn north, when I saw the tiny speck of rock and white water in the far distance to the south.

John Stout had been the Depot Manager for thirty years when he retired in 1997. In his early years as Assistant Manager, he was also available as an 'emergency occasional light-keeper'. He never became interested in becoming a *bona fide* light-keeper, probably because of his few emergency experiences at lighthouses.

One episode involved being sent to Westray's Noup Head Lighthouse. The tower stands on the edge of a high cliff which juts like a gnarled finger out into the Atlantic. John took over the light with another keeper from Dunnet Head for ten days over Christmas, while the usual light-house crew, and most of the islanders, were down with flu. A rope from the keepers' quarters to the tower door acted as a life-line to hold on to when the Atlantic Storms raged so hard they could pluck you out of the courtyard.

Top *Stromness Depot pier and the* Fingal

Left *Buoys, Stromness Depot*

Bottom *Cape Wrath keeper, Ron Nixon, at the Stromness helicopter pad with supplies for his four weeks on the rock*

Opposite *John Stout, Depot Manager*

BROUGH OF BIRSAY

Birsay was the poet George Mackay Brown's favourite Orkney parish. Its fertile fields and sea-bird cliffs are delightful in summer.

With the Brough's Attendant Keeper, Benny Norquoy, I visited the lighthouse on a sunny, breezy August day. With the tide out, we crossed the causeway to the island and walked up the gentle, sea-pink slopes, past ruins of Viking settlements; the Brough was an important base for Norse Earls from around 800 AD to the 12th century.

Up at the lighthouse, a curious castellated affair on the edge of a high cliff, we stopped to take in the view. It was just off the Brough that Lord Kitchener, First Lord of the Admiralty, died in 1916 when, on route to Russia, his ship hit a mine and sank almost immediately.

Fulmars, stiff-winged and beady-eyed, glided past us as I took some portraits of Benny standing beside the tower.

Established	1925
Automated	Built as automatic
Engineer	David A. Stevenson
Character	Flashing 3 white every 25 sec
Range	18 miles

NOUP HEAD

A nother Orkney name of Norse origin, 'Noup' is derived from *gnupr*, meaning high headland. The lighthouse stands on this headland, marking the spectacular end of a five-mile stretch of cliffs which in places reach over 300 feet above sea level.

Every Monday, since December 1964, Gavin Seatter, a Pierowall crofter, has driven the five miles with his wife to Noup Head Lighthouse to maintain and clean the place. The occasional storm can keep him busy too: 'We had four lantern panes broken on four occasions in one winter,' said Gavin. The storms had ripped stone slabs off the cliffs below and dashed them against the tower.

Apart from that winter, Gavin's routine has continued more or less uninterrupted. There has been only one occasion, he told me, when the Commissioners have inspected, during his time with the light: 'It was all right when the visit was over,' he said.

These high Westray cliffs attract tens of thousands of sea birds each summer. The ledges are ideal for nesting, and it has been a tradition here for local people to take a small number of birds and their eggs. Two crofters showed me the way down to sea level at a point about 200 yards from the lighthouse. We followed a series of ledges which led, one after the other via rough steps, down to the final ledge which led into the Gentleman's Cave, one of a group of cliff-caves on Westray where islanders were able to hide from the press gangs in the 18th and early 19th centuries.

Above *Gavin Seatter, Noup Head*

Established	1898
Automated	1964
Engineer	David A. Stevenson
Character	Flashing white every 30 sec
Range	22 miles

CALF OF EDAY

This neat little tower is named after the uninhabited island opposite. The lighthouse was built to assist Orkney's North Isles boats, which carried passengers and cargo between Kirkwall and Westray. The route took in Calf Sound, as the ships almost completed their journeys before reaching their final destination for the day, Westray.

Many islands were visited on the way from Kirkwall, and the whole trip, starting at 6.00 am, must have been the most scenic in Scotland.

The shore opposite the lighthouse, on the Calf of Eday itself, is famous in Orkney as the site of the notorious pirate John Gow's shipwreck in 1725 – well, the lighthouse wasn't yet built. Gow was captured and held in the Laird's mansion, Carrick House, near the Calf Sound shore. Sir Walter Scott later based his novel *The Pirate* on the John Gow adventure, and Daniel Defoe published an account of it.

I was invited for lunch with the Joys of Carrick House, and afterwards was shown the pirate's blood-stains on their sitting-room floorboards.

Left *Calf of Eday Light*

The Joys of Carrick House

Right *Attendant Keeper Malcolm Scott*

Established	1909
Automated	Built as automatic
Engineer	David A. Stevenson
Character	Isophase wht/red/grn every 5 sec
Range	Wht 8/red 7/grn 6 miles

NORTH RONALDSAY

I first set foot on North Ronaldsay as a Roving Keeper in 1975, when '84' posted me here for four weeks. The helicopter flew me out from Stromness on that beautiful April morning – over the moors and farms of the Orkney Mainland, over Eday, and over the long white beaches of Sanday.

As we approached North Ronaldsay, all we could see was a thin white veil of fog clinging to the island, and the tall brick tower (Britain's tallest land-based lighthouse) protruding through it.

We circled the tower a couple of times – to look at the surreal sight – and being unable to land, headed north to Fair Isle and Bressay where a Superintendent from '84', who was also on board the helicopter, had 'some business' to sort out.

A few hours later, we were flying south, and by the time we reached North Ronaldsay again, the fog had cleared and I was landed.

North Ronaldsay measures four miles by two, and around 80 people live here, mostly crofting and fishing. It is the northernmost of the Orkney islands, and lies quite apart from the rest. A salty, remote feeling seems to hang around the place. A high dry-stone wall completely surrounds the island, which keeps the small hardy North Ronaldsay sheep on the shore, where they survive by eating seaweed.

The 'new light', as it is called here, was built in 1854 to replace one of the Board's first four lights in Scotland – which still stands, about 500 yeards east of the new light. Ravens were nesting on a window-ledge of the old light when I first came here.

Established	1854 (previous tower 1789-1809)
Automated	1998
Engineer	Thomas Smith
Character	Flashing white every 10 sec
Range	19 miles

Above *Billy Muir in the lens*
Below *North Ronaldsay keepers and their families*

The new light has 176 steps from the base to the light-room. More than once as a keeper here I ran fast, non-stop, up these steps when I sometimes misjudged the winding time. If I left the winding just a little late, then a weight, which slowly descended the tower (as in a grand-father clock system) would push a lever down and trigger very loud alarm bells around the station. I can still remember the sensational relief at reaching the light-room, grabbing the winding-handle, and turning it with only seconds to spare.

The lighthouse at this time employed four full-time keepers and four part-time keepers. Billy Muir, a native of North Ronaldsay, was the Local Assistant Keeper. He reminded me that when I first came here, the keepers would do the 'message round', delivering groceries twice a week to about ten crofts (as well as to the lighthouse).

I can still see Billy now approaching a croft door, while chickens, and a couple of cats, a goat and a cow would wander over to investigate him; and with the door

Above *The original North Ronaldsay lighthhouse*
Below *A decorated ventilator cover in the light-room*

opening, an old lady appearing with two dogs to complete the assembly.

My posting to North Ronaldsay then was partly due to one of the light-keepers, Bill Edwardson, being away on holiday. 'In his youth, he was the sort of keeper,' someone told me, 'who would come back from an island dance and "see a girl home", and at five to two in the morning climb into his house through a back window, and appear at his front door a minute later, ready to meet the PLK to take over from his watch.'

The last three families at North Ronaldsay will leave the lighthouse when the station is automated in March 1998. There will be no ceremony, but just feelings of regret when it happens. The Paynes will leave for Kirkwall, while the Craigies and Hendersons will stay on the island.

SHETLAND

FAIR ISLE SOUTH

With Assistant Light-keeper Jock Stevenson, I flew in the NLB helicopter from Stromness to Fair Isle on the fortnightly relief. Within hours of landing, fog closed in, and my planned two-day visit turned into a five-day visit.

My accommodation was at the lighthouse with the three keepers; there were plenty of spare rooms, as originally this had been a three-family station.

Jim Watt, another Assistant Keeper at the Fair Isle, lived here first with his wife and children in the early 1970s, since when he has had three shifts before returning, finally, to Fair Isle. His own former family quarters are now the three-man quarters of the lighthouse.

For two years prior to automation, teams of builders, joiners, electricians and technicians have worked at the lighthouse, sharing the place with the keepers. And once all the preparation has been completed, the station will be closed, and 211 years of light-keepers with the NLB will come to an end.

'I'll be the last keeper to leave the lighthouse,' said Angus Hutchinson, the other PLK, who was spending his 'ashore' time at home with his wife in Stromness during my Fair Isle visit. 'And I'll turn the key and lock the lighthouse door on the last day of March 1998.'

A small ceremony will be held at the lighthouse on that

day, and another lighthouse name and number will appear on the Monitor Centre computer screen at '84'. 'It's sad,' said Angus, 'but someone had to be the last. I've had 36 years in the service, and it's held my security over the years. But I'm sad that younger men can't carry on the tradition.'

Angus met his wife Yvonne at Rubh' Re, on the north-west coast of Scotland; it was his first lighthouse. They married there in the early 1960s and had two children. The other two keepers had young wives too, and with the light-keeping came the lasting friendships which can develop amongst lighthouse families. The way of life also brought the pleasures of keeping hens, and cutting peat at their own peat-banks, going for walks and even playing rounders in that remote outpost.

Established	1892
Automated	1998 (the last manned in Scotland)
Engineer	David A. Stevenson
Character	Flashing 4 white every 30 sec
Range	24 miles

Annie and Stewart Thomson

ALK Jock Stevenson

Then came other moves for Angus and his family, as all light-keepers are usually moved to a new light every five years: to Sule Skerry (six weeks 'on the rock' and three weeks off), then to Noss Head, near Wick, and then promotion to PLK on Stroma. Then to Fair Isle when it was a family station, followed by the Point of Ayre on the Isle of Man, and finally back to Fair Isle. 'I was devastated when we got word to leave the Isle of Man,' said Yvonne. 'I was working in Ramsay at an old people's home, a small place of only twelve people, but I loved them...'

I met Stewart and Annie Thomson of Shirva, a croft about a mile from the South Light while on a drive around Fair Isle with Frank Bremner, the PLK. Stewart first came to Fair Isle as a keeper during the Second World War, when his accommodation was a Nissen hut near the lighthouse. The keepers' quarters of the South Light had suffered a direct hit during a German bombing raid only a few months earlier, killing the PLK's wife and child, and a soldier manning a machine-gun post.

Stewart's job was to switch the light on and off at certain times for brief periods only, following military orders by phone. One night, Stewart told me, he received an urgent call: 'For God's sake, will you put the light on – there's a ship heading for you!' Immediately Stewart ran to the fog-horn while another keeper ran to the lantern. The lighting-up was a relatively slow procedure, but as the great optics started to revolve and the first beams swept over the sea, the keepers were shocked to see a troop ship dangerously close to the island. The light shone in time to prevent a disaster. Stewart learned later that the ship was carrying 1,000 troops.

FAIR ISLE NORTH

I went to the north light every day with Frank in the lighthouse Landrover. Sometimes John or Jim would come too, just to look around, and maybe see if any unusual birds had landed. Mostly just to fill in the time.

The keepers' quarters were removed a few years after automation. The outline of the foundations was still clearly visible.

Later, looking at an early copy of the NLB Journal (summer 1974), I found an article by a former keeper:

'October saw the start of the gales with a N.W. beauty… Christmas Eve was the first time we had carol singers at the station… and guisers at Hogmanay.

'The Burns Supper held at the nurses' home was well attended, the address to the haggis being given by Jimmy 'Midway' who seemed to be thankful when it was all over… '

Established	1892
Automated	1998
Engineer	David A. Stevenson
Character	Flashing 2 white every 30 sec
Range	22 miles

Below *Interior of the engine room, Fair Isle North*

SUMBURGH HEAD

Eilean Leask has been the Attendant to Sumburgh Head since the light's automation in 1991. She was far from new to the service as her husband, Jimmy (now retired), had been a keeper since 1970. Their first lighthouse together was Holy Island, when it was a family station. For a while, Eilean was the only woman on the island, as the other two keepers were single men.

The RSPB's Shetland HQ now occupies the former PLK's house at Sumburgh Lighthouse, while the Assistant's quarters are holiday accommodation. A few visitors were exploring the place and climbing around the fog-horn tower when I arrived.

By chance I met a whale-watcher, Howard Loates, at the lighthouse. He reckoned that Sumburgh Head is one of Europe's best whale-watching sites. He has seen a huge hump-back whale scratching itself on a rock below the lighthouse, and has often seen killer whales attacking

seals. His notes make fascinating reading for Sumburgh Head:

12th June, 19.30 hours (1996): '… in my car at Sumburgh Head, when tall fins came into view heading north in the tide-way… a bull killer whale with three cows and a fairly large calf swam by… I dashed to the promontory just in time to see them approach a

Established	1821
Automated	1991
Engineer	Robert Stevenson
Character	Flashing 3 white every 30 sec
Range	23 miles

large sloping rock almost directly underneath me. Three of the animals including the bull then swam up the rock so that half their bodies were clear of the water for a quick look around before sliding back into the water.'

23rd June, 14.00 hours (1996): … 'the whales travelled towards me very close to the shore… milled around about 40 metres out, with one of the females swimming on her back with pectoral fins above the water, then the bull disappeared. At this time, the seals appeared unconcerned… With gasps from the assembled watchers, the bull blasted out from nowhere at full speed and lunged at a seal, and they were both lost from view… blood and flesh were seen in the water, and gulls and maulies gathered for a feast.'

I camped on the shores of West Voe of Sumburgh, across the bay from the lighthouse. I sat on the sea-pink turf near my tent watching the lighthouse beams reflect on a perfectly still sea while an otter slowly explored the seaweed below me.

Above *Attendant Keeper Eilean Leask*
Below *Abandoned fog-horn compressors*

MOUSA

Above *John William Smith, attendant to Mousa lighthouse*

J ust off Mousa's eastern shores lies a holm called Peerie Bard on which stands Mousa Lighthouse.

Mousa itself is famous for its ancient broch, a full Iron-age stone-built tower, in which people could shelter from attack; it is the best preserved of Scotland's 500 or so known broch sites.

But Mousa is also becoming well-known for its breeding storm-petrels. They nest in the crevices of the broch, and around other parts of the island's shore; each night in the summer, these nocturnal sea birds, like dainty house-martins, flutter around the island. I saw many storm-petrels on Sule Skerry when I was Local Assistant Keeper there in the 1970s. The ornithologist and writer R.M. Lockley, calls these birds the storm fairies, and his daughter, when she was very young, described their strange call as a long churring, followed by the sound of a fairy being sick.

Once a fortnight since 1972, John William Smith has been attending Mousa Lighthouse. In his time, he has also been Local Assistant, then Occasional Keeper, to Sumburgh Head Lighthouse until its automation in 1991.

John has a beautiful 50-year-old fishing boat, with which he sets creels for crabs and lobsters around Mousa. Usually, one of his five sons accompanies him in the *Victory II*, to help with the boat during the lighthouse inspections.

Below *John rowing his boat with* Victory II *behind him*

Established	1951
Automated	Built as automatic
Engineer	P. H. Hyslop
Character	Flashing white every 3 seconds
Range	10 miles

FUGLA NESS

I took the steep road out of Lerwick and travelled west for Hamnavoe and the Fugla Ness lighthouse. At the village, I met Walter and Mimie Smith. Walter is the Light's Attendant. Mimie was too, in her time, before the light was modernised. 'There's no brass any more,' she told me. 'It went with the old lens about ten years ago.' Walter and Mimie used to go to the old light together once a fortnight. And if it was painting time, then they would take a picnic and make a day of it. 'We'd have an early start, then light a fire and have our picnic lunch, and sleep for an hour, then carry on till 8 or 9 at night,' said Mimie.

Walter and I went to the lighthouse, following the Hamnavoe shore. He knew every rock and stone. 'Under that rock, there are otters,' he said, and near the light he pointed out huge slabs which the previous winter's storms had shifted (and he pointed out exactly where they had been moved from).

The next day I walked to the Clift Hills, more or less following the Burn of Laxdale from the main road. Foula was poking through a thick wad of fog, while over to the north-west, Fugla Ness was just visible amongst a vast landscape of alternating rock and water.

Established	1893
Automated	Built as automatic
Engineer	David A. Stevenson
Character	Flashing 2 wht/red/grn every 10 sec
Range	Wht 10/red 7/grn 7 miles

BRESSAY

One of the most fascinating boat trips in Scotland is Jonathan Wills' summer tour from Lerwick, down the Bressay Sound and around Bressay's southern tip, then over to the Isle of Noss. The climax of the trip is finding a spot under the 1,000 foot high cliffs, sea-bird cities of guillemots and gannets, and switching off the boat's engine. Then great rafts of guillemots lose their fear and become inquisitive, paddling closer to the boat until you can almost touch them.

On the way back from Noss, Jonathan nosed the boat in around the cliffs below Bressay Lighthouse. He knows the name and its meaning of every bit of cliff and cove around this part of the coast. We crept into a cave and stared into the clear water to watch the astonishing colours of sea anemones.

Established	1858
Automated	1989
Engineer	David & Thomas Stevenson
Character	Flashing 2 white every 20 sec
Range	23 miles

MULL OF ESWICK

R aymond Robertson and his son Mark had spent 'three painting years' with the Mull of Eswick minor light before it vanished into the sea, along with a huge chunk of Shetland coast with it. The 1908 tower, complete with the lighthouse shed (a worthy pieces of architecture too), fell into the sea on 5th November 1994.

A new light, using solar energy, has replaced the old – on a square aluminium and steel frame.

Raymond showed me the new light, and he pointed out the piece of cliff which had collapsed – then we went back to Langness, his home a mile along the road, for a huge breakfast. Raymond's wife had prepared freshly baked bannocks and great mugs of tea.

I read the Monthly Return Book for the original Eswick Light, which Raymond keeps in his kitchen. It details the cleaning and oiling of the original paraffin light every three or four days, with daily reports. The letter written after the first night of lighting read: 'On the 1st, exhibited light according to instructions. Light satisfactory, revolving apparatus not satisfactory showing from 4 to 9 flashes per minute, according to direction of wind.'

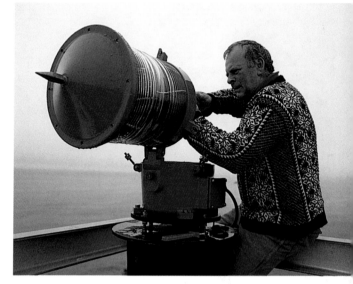

Above *Raymond Robertson on top of the light*

Established	1904
Automated	Built as automatic
Engineer	David A. Stevenson
Character	Flashing wht/red/grn every 3 sec
Range	Wht 9/red 6/grn 6 miles

LUNNA HOLM

The Robertsons

With the development of the oil industry in Shetland in the 1970s, the Lunna Holm light was only one of a string of new lights constructed on strategic rocks around the islands.

Eddie Dishon, an '84' technician, who installed the optic, recalled how his hands were so numb from the cold when he was working at the new light that he could hardly turn a spanner. Even the sea was frozen in the voes that winter.

I met the Attendant Keeper and his wife, the Robertsons, at their house on the Vidlin Voe shore just half an hour before they left Shetland for their annual holiday.

This is 'Shetland Bus' country: Lunna House, on the Lunna Ness peninsula (which culminates in Lunna Holm), was the HQ of the famous Shetland–Norway boat link during the Second World War. The book *The Shetland Bus*, written by Lt Commander David Howarth, has a foreword which explains: During the German occupation of Norway, from 1940 to 1945, every Norwegian knew that small boats were constantly sailing from the Shetland Isles to Norway, to land weapons and supplies, and to rescue refugees...'

Established	1985
Automated	Built as automatic
Engineer	J. H. K. Williamson
Character	Flashing 3 wht/red/grn every 15 sec
Range	Wht 10/red 7/grn 7 miles

FIRTH'S VOE

Lolly Blance beneath Firth's Voe lighthouse

I found Lolly Blance at his croft on the Shetland mainland shore of Yell Sound. His cottage is only two small fields away from the light. He is the latest in a long line of Blances who have been Attendant Keepers at Firth's Voe since the light's construction in 1909.

We walked to the lighthouse in the rain – it had been raining for over two days now – crossed a small pasture sprinkled with yellow irises, and then went through a little field of sodden hay. The only colour on the shore was Lolly's oilskin.

Established	1909
Automated	Built as automatic
Engineer	David A. Stevenson
Character	Occulting wht/red/grn every 8 sec
Range	Wht 15/red 10/grn 10 miles

OUT SKERRIES

In order to visit Out Skerries Lighthouse, I had to do a bit of island hopping. First, having arrived at Lerwick, Shetland's main town, I took the three-hour ferry crossing to the handful of islands called Out Skerries, far out to the north-east of the Shetland island group.

Just after arriving, I bumped into the Attendant Keeper to the Out Skerries light, Bobby Johnstone, in the islands shop. We'd met before on my previous visit to Out Skerries, working on the first volume of *At Scotland's Edge*. The next day Bobby took me in his boat over to the tiny island called Grunay, ten minutes from the Out Skerries harbour, where the keepers' quarters stand empty and neglected.

On my earlier visit, an English couple were living here, having bought the houses with the island. But the isolation was troubling them, and it didn't surprise me that they didn't stay long. Since then, the houses have been wrecked by storms and damp.

Then Bobby took me over to the lighthouse island, Bound Skerry, about half a mile from the keepers' cottages. An old railway line from the jetty to the light-house lay derelict, and a pair of greater black-backed gulls repeatedly swooped over us as we looked around. We opened the door, and climbed the vertical ladder inside

Established	1854
Automated	1972
Engineer	David & Thomas Stevenson
Character	Flashing white every 20 sec
Range	20 miles

which had replaced the series of angled steps which formerly linked the floors. We passed each room, while Bobby told me about their functions – first, the oil cellar, then the water-tank room, then store room, workshop, kitchen and bedroom; then came, after reaching a landing, the light-room and ultimately the lantern. (The toilet was in a little shed outside on the rocks.)

Bobby had been stationed here during the war, before his sixteenth birthday. He was here with another Out Skerries islander, Lolly Anderson, who was just over sixteen at the time.

Sea mines had been a problem out here. But the two lads had a .303 rifle, which had lain jammed for several months. After repairing it, Lolly said, 'Bobby, if only we could see a mine,' and Bobby looked out of the kitchen window and said, 'Lolly, I see a mine!' So they fired at the mine and eventually they hit it and it exploded.

During their time at Out Skerries lighthouse, they saw a German plane circle Grunay twice, before it dropped a bomb right inside one of the keepers' houses. The Attending Boatman's mother was in the house at the time, and was killed instantly.

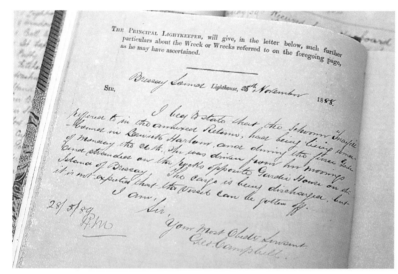

Left *The keepers' shipwreck return book*
Below *Bobby Johnstone, Lolly Anderson and Donny Hendersdon*

ESHA NESS

*Leslie Johnson,
Attendant Keeper at
Esha Ness*

Esha Ness might seem the last place on earth in which most people would choose to retire. It is one of Shetland's remotest out-posts, a great finger of rock poking into the Atlantic Ocean, on the end of which clings, like a limpet, Esha Ness Lighthouse.

I visited the light with the Attendant Keeper, Leslie Johnson, and called on Rian and Sandra James who have bought the keeper's quarters. They are retired, and have renovated the place themselves, keeping the atmosphere of a light-keeper's house by caring about the details – the wooden window-shutters, the magnificent doors, and the fireplaces. And outside, the place is as immaculate as when a keeper lived here. The paint-work is sparkling white, the lawns closely mown, the Union Flag is flying. A tame herring gull is sitting on a fence-post, and the James' maroon Rolls Royce stands gleaming in the drive.

In the cosy sitting room, over drams of whisky, it is easy to feel the strong sense of security and home which the James have created here. But Leslie told us a story he had heard from his father (who was an Occasional Keeper here) when a winter storm had thrown 20 barrow loads of rocks onto the roof and the courtyard. A stone even reached the lantern, smashing one of the panes,

almost 200 hundred feet above sea level, and one rock on the roof of the house was so big it took two men to shift it. The roof of the house, Rian assured us, was strong enough to stand up to anything thrown at it – the roof is made of thick concrete, 'as strong as a motorway'.

I read later an engineers' report in the NLB Journal, dated 1974, about the alterations work: 'The most difficult part of the work was the cutting of a new entrance door to the tower, which is reinforced concrete. It was found that steel chains had been embedded in the concrete and the cutting of the new door took almost four weeks.'

Established	1929
Automated	1974
Engineer	David A. Stevenson
Character	Flashing white every 12 sec
Range	25 miles

POINT OF FETHALAND

The Point of Fethaland Lighthouse stands on the northernmost point of Shetland's mainland. This area, Isbister, is farmed by Douglas and Bertha Murray – and Douglas is the Attendant Keeper to the light. I was invited into the farmhouse for a cup of tea before setting off to the lighthouse – in the kitchen a Raeburn belted out heat and pairs of hooded crows' wings hung on the walls, drying out in preparation for the Up Helly A, the mid-winter fire ceremony (the smaller North Marine Festival, rather than the Lerwick festival).

On the way to the Point of Fethaland, we passed the ruins of a croft – where Douglas was brought up. His father, he told me, always had a lamp burning in the porch, in full view of Yell Sound for the benefit of the fishermen, and always believed that one day a lighthouse would be built around here. With the arrival of the oil industry in Shetland in the 1970s, a lighthouse was indeed built on the Point of Fethaland. It was first lit in 1978, with electricity directly from the Hydro-Board.

Established	1977
Automated	1977 (built as an automatic)
Engineer	P. H. Hyslop
Character	Flashing 3 white/red every 20 sec
Range	White 24 miles, red 20 miles

Douglas Murray, Attendant Keeper

UYEA SOUND

Robert Hughson is only the second Attendant to the Uyea Sound Light since its construction in 1946. The light was needed mainly for the assistance of the *Earl of Zetland*, a freight and tourist ship which sailed between Lerwick and Unst. But although the *Earl* stopped sailing in 1972, the light has continued to be maintained.

Robert's grandfather was a shepherd on Uyea Island earlier this century, just half a mile off Unst opposite the light. He had a family of eight on the island, and between the World Wars he kept a lamp burning every Sunday night in his house in a window at the head of the stair to assist the passage of the *Earl of Zetland*.

Established	1946
Automated	Built as automatic
Engineer	J. A. Gardner
Character	Flashing 2 white every 8 sec
Range	7 miles

BALTA SOUND

Attendant Keeper Christopher Ritch

Christopher Ritch took over as Attendant Keeper to the Balta Sound light in 1994 following the death of his father. His great-grandfather was the first Attendant, taking up the post in 1895.

The lighthouse has always been a minor automatic light, though in the early years when it ran on paraffin, and later carbide, calling it automatic was not quite accurate.

In fact, the light needed so much attention in the early years that Christopher's great-grandfather built a wooden bothy in Balta to shelter in during rough weather, and to spend the night if he was caught out by a rough sea. Christopher and I looked inside the bothy. A window had blown in, and scattered over the floor lay a kettle and a small blue teapot, a bread knife and a plate. An otter, long dead, lay in a corner, its white skull bulging through its black skin.

The island of Balta is uninhabited, though around the turn of the century it was a bustling herring station each summer. There are ruined jetties and the foundations of scores of vanished buildings along the shore on the bay side. At the height of the fishing industry, there could

have been over five thousand people living and working on Balta, the northernmost outpost of the migrant workers who followed the herring along the east coast of Scotland and the Northern Isles.

Christopher is co-owner of a salmon farm in the Baltasound Bay. Without the salmon farm, he would not be living in Unst – he would have planned a career in Environmental Science following his degree course at Stirling University.

Established	1895
Automated	Built as automatic
Engineer	David A. Stevenson
Character	Flashing white/red every 10 sec
Range	White 10 miles, red 7 miles

MUCKLE FLUGGA

I parked my car at the old shore station by Burra Firth, in Shetland's most northerly island, most northerly except for the line of jagged rocks which stand about three miles, as the crow flies, north of the shore station. Muckle Flugga is the name of the biggest of the rocks, and it is on this one that the lighthouse stands. 'Big bird island' is the translation of the Norse name Muckle Flugga. But all the birds – gannets, thousands of them – swarmed over the other rocks next to Muckle Flugga. I could see them from my vantage point on the edge of the cliff at Herma Ness, the most northerly tip of Unst.

Great banks of fog swirled up from the Atlantic to the west and occasionally hid Muckle Flugga. As darkness was beginning to fall, I stumbled back south over the two miles of bog and heather to the Burra Firth shore station. (I was attacked by bonxies, the big dark menacing northern gulls otherwise called great skuas, as I passed through their territories and near their nests.)

North Unst and Muckle Flugga are 'the bitter end of Britain', according to journalist Jonathan Wills (an ex-Muckle Flugga Attending Boatman). In the 1970s he'd take the boat, the *Grace Darling*, from the shore station out to the Flugga with his six-man crew for the reliefs:

'The landing was always tricky,' said Jonathan. 'There was no room for error. The boat to landing distance – over 10 feet. Keepers were usually hauled up by block and tackle. Sometimes, just for a laugh, a new keeper would be given a ducking before we handed him up to the landing.'

Established	1854
Automated	1995
Engineer	Thomas and David Stevenson
Character	Flashing white every 20 sec
Range	22 miles

'Then there were the keepers' belongings – we took it all by boat – even a Ferguson tractor was taken out, piece by piece, over a few months. The keeper used all his free time to do it up that way!'

The shore station has now been sold by the NLB since Muckle Flugga was automated. There are four flats, and one of them has been bought by an ex-keeper, Lawrence Johnstone. He now works for Bristows at Unst Airport.

The PLK's flat at the shore station has been taken over by Scottish National Heritage, where their Herma Ness Reserve warden lives, and where an exhibition is housed. When visitors enter the PLK's former sitting room, they can press buttons to create the sounds of skuas, gannets and guillemots. The raucous calls echo through all the flats in the building.

Opposite *Muckle Flugga from Barra Firth*
Above *Muckle Flugga Shore Station*
Below *Puffin, Herma Ness*

LIGHTHOUSE
MUSEUMS

Scotland's Lighthouse Museum
Kinnaird Head
Fraserburgh
Aberdeenshire
AB43 9DU

Tel. 01346 511022
Fax   01346 511033

Scotland's Lighthouse Museum opened in June 1995. It has an extensive collection of lighthouse artefacts from all over Scotland mainly donated by the Northern Lighthouse Board. This unique collection is on display in a purpose-built museum. Visitors can stroll through the display of major and minor lenses reassembled on the ground floor of the museum before watching our audio visual presentation 'The Northern Lights'. The museum also contains a display dedicated to lighthouse engineering and the remarkable story of the Stevenson family.

There is a temporary exhibition area with a changing programme of displays. A library and study area contains the largest collection of lighthouse-related books, documents, postcards and photographs anywhere in Scotland.

The jewel in the crown of the museum is Kinnaird Head Lighthouse itself. Standing just 50 metres across the headland from the museum, the lighthouse was the first built by the Northern Lighthouse Board in 1787. The station was automated in 1991 when a new light was built just in front of the original tower. The original light, built inside a castle tower, was left intact exactly as it was the day the last lighthouse keeper left. Visitors are taken on a unique guided tour right to the very top of the tower and into the lantern itself. The view from the balcony is always impressive.

The Museum also includes a café and a shop stocking a range of lighthouse books, postcards and souvenirs.

Open all year   **1st April – end of October**
Monday – Saturday 10.00 am – 6.00 pm
Sunday 12.00 pm – 6.00pm

1st November – end of March
Monday – Saturday 10.00 am – 4.00 pm
Sunday 12.00 pm – 4.00 pm

Ardnamurchan Visitor Centre
Kilchoan, Ardnamurchan,
Argyll,
PH36 4LN

Tel. 01972 510210

The former lighthouse buildings have been developed into a innovative visitor centre which uses video and computer technology to illustrate the history and science of lighthouses. Visitors can see the original lens, the engine room which operated the foghorn and listen to radio conversations of the keeper's.

Two keeper's cottages have been restored and offer high quality, self-catering accommodation. Café, gift shop and children's play area are available.

Open 1st April to 31st October, 10 am – 6 pm (5 pm in October). Admission charge.

National Museums of Scotland
Chambers St,
Edinburgh,
EH1 1JF

Tel. 0131 247 4219

NMS holds an important collection of lighthouse optics and engineering items. Robert Stevenson's large model of his Bell Rock Lighthouse will be in the new Museum of Scotland (level 4) and the first order optic from Inchkeith in the West Hall of the Royal Museum, both open from December 1998. The re-displayed Lighthouse Gallery in the Royal Museum is due to open in 1999.

Gairloch Heritage Museum
Achtercairn,
Gairloch,
Ross-shire,
IV21 2BJ

Tel. 01445 712287

On display from the local lighthouse, Rudha Reidh, is the lens with its huge glass reflectors and prisms, one of the largest ever made. The original fog-horn is re-erected outside and its actuating mechanism is shown. Archive material on the history of the lighthouse may be consulted by prior arrangement.

Signal Tower Museum
Ladyloan,
Arbroath,
Angus,
DD11 1PU

Tel. 01241 875598

Arbroath Museum is housed in the Signal Tower and shore station for Robert Stevenson's famed Bell Rock Lighthouse, 11.5 miles off shore. The last manually operated light and lenses from the Bell Rock are brought to life with a talking life-size model lighthouse keeper. The feat of constructing the lighthouse and the life of the lighthouse keepers and their families is told in this elegant Regency complex.

Open Mon–Sat 10 am to 5 pm all year and Sun 2 pm–5 pm July and August. Admission free.

Stromness Museum
52 Alfred Street,
Stromness,
Orkney,
KW16 3DF

Tel. 01856 850025

Orkney has 11 major and 11 minor lighthouses, by far the largest number in any Scottish county. The exhibition at Stromness Museum tells their story through photographs and text. Among the artefacts on display is the catadioptric lens from Hoy Sound (Low), and memorabilia of the keepers and their families.

Places to Stay

There are a number of lighthouse keepers' cottages around the Scottish coast which have been converted to holiday accommodation. These can be found at

Corsewell Point
Neist Point
Sumburgh Head
Cantick Head
Rubha Reidh

Scotland's Lighthouse Museum will be happy to supply on request a leaflet it produces giving details of places to see and places to stay all around Scotland.

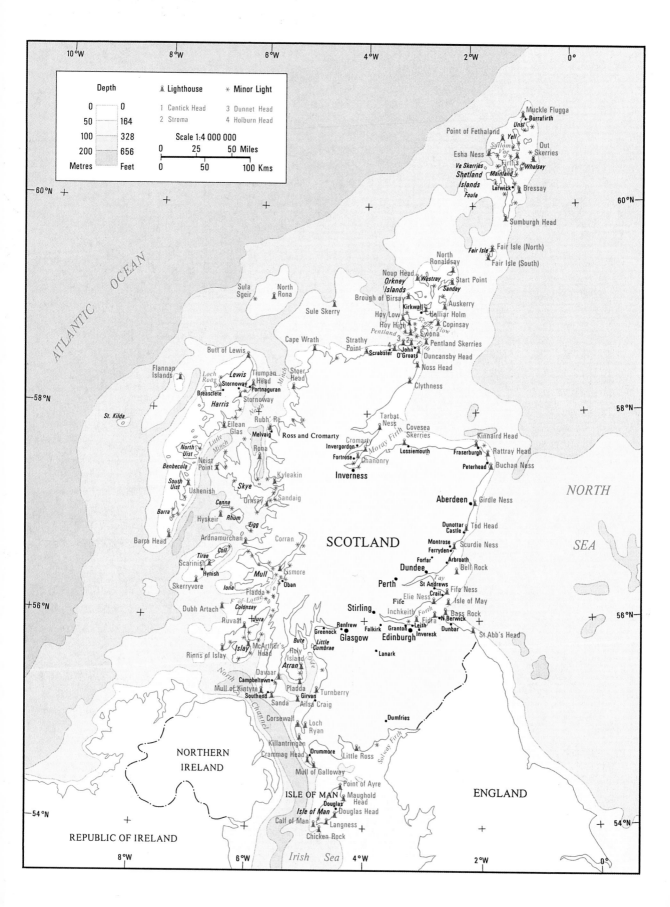

Depth

0	0
50	164
100	328
200	656
Metres	Feet

⚓ Lighthouse   ✴ Minor Light

1 Cantick Head   3 Dunnet Head
2 Stroma   4 Holburn Head

Scale 1:4 000 000

0   25   50 Miles

0   50   100 Kms

10°W   8°W   6°W   4°W   2°W   0°

ATLANTIC OCEAN

Muckle Flugga
Burrafirth
Point of Fethaland   Unst
Esha Ness   Yell   Out Skerries
Ve Skerries   Sullom Voe
Shetland Islands   Mainland   Whalsay
Foula   Lerwick   Bressay

60°N   60°N

Sumburgh Head

Fair Isle   Fair Isle (North)
Fair Isle (South)

Sula Sgeir   North Rona
North Ronaldsay
Noup Head   Westray   Start Point
Sule Skerry   Orkney Islands   Sanday
Brough of Birsay   Auskerry
Kirkwall   Halliar Holm   Copinsay
Hoy Low   Hoy High   Scapa Flow   Wona
Cape Wrath   Pentland Skerries
Strathy Point   Pentland Firth
Scrabster   John   Duncansby Head
O'Groats   Noss Head

Butt of Lewis
Flannan Islands   Tiumpan Head   Stoer Head   Clythness
Loch Roag   Lewis   Stornoway
58°N   Breasclete   Portnaguran   58°N
Harris   Stornoway
St. Kilda   Rubh' Re   Tarbat Ness
Eilean Glas   Melvaig   Covesea Skerries   Kinnaird Head
North Uist   Rona   Ross and Cromarty   Lossiemouth   Fraserburgh   Rattray Head
Little Minch   Cromarty   Peterhead   Buchan Ness
Benbecula   Neist Point   Invergordon
South Uist   Fortrose   Chanonry
Barra   Ushenish   Skye   Inverness
Orksay   Sandaig   Aberdeen   Girdle Ness
Canna   Kyleakin
Hyskeir   Rhum   Eigg
Barra Head   Ardnamurchan   Corran   Dunottar Castle   Tod Head
Tiree   Coll   Montrose   Scurdie Ness
Scarinish   SCOTLAND   Forfar   Ferryden
Hynish   Mull   Lismore   Oban   Dundee   Arbroath   Bell Rock
Skerryvore   Iona   Perth   St Andrews   Fife Ness
Fladda   Elie Ness   Crail   Isle of May
Dubh Artach   F. of Lorne   Colonsay   Fife   Bass Rock
56°N   Ruvaal   Jura   Stirling   Inchkeith   Forth   Fidra   56°N
Renfrew   Falkirk   Granton   N. Berwick
Greenock   Leith   Dunbar
Islay   McArthur's Head   Bute   Glasgow   Edinburgh   Inveresk
Rinns of Islay   Holy Island   Little Cumbrae   St Abb's Head
Arran   Lanark
Davaar
Campbeltown   Pladda   Turnberry
Mull of Kintyre   Girvan   Dumfries
Southend   Sanda   Ailsa Craig
Corsewall   Loch Ryan   Solway Firth
North Channel   Killantringan
Crammag Head   Drummore   Little Ross
Mull of Galloway

NORTH SEA

NORTHERN IRELAND

ENGLAND

Point of Ayre   Maughold Head
ISLE OF MAN   Douglas
Isle of Man   Douglas Head
54°N   Calf of Man   Langness   54°N
Chicken Rock

REPUBLIC OF IRELAND

Irish Sea

8°W   6°W   4°W   2°W   0°

128